THE SECRET
NORTHERN SHAOLIN KUNG-FU

The History, Form, and Function of
PEK SIL LUM

THE SECRETS OF
NORTHERN SHAOLIN KUNG-FU

The History, Form, and Function of
PEK SIL LUM

Lai Hung and
Brian Klingborg

Tuttle Publishing
Boston • Rutland, Vermont • Tokyo

Disclaimer

Please note that the author and publisher of this book are NOT RESPONSIBLE in any manner whatsoever for any injury that may result from practicing the techniques and/or following the instructions given within. Since the physical activities described herein may be too strenuous in nature for some readers to engage in safely, it is essential that a physician be consulted prior to training.

First published in 1999 by Tuttle Publishing, an imprint of Periplus Editions (HK) Ltd., with editorial offices at 153 Milk Street, Boston, Massachusetts 02109.
Copyright © 1999 by Brian Klingborg

All rights reserved. No part of this publication may be reproduced or utilized in any form or by any means, electronic or mechanical, including photocopying, recording, or by any information storage and retrieval system, without prior written permission from Tuttle Publishing.

LIBRARY OF CONGRESS CATALOGING-IN-PUBLICATION DATA
Klingborg, Brian, 1967
  The Secrets of Northern Shaolin Kung-Fu: the history, form, and function of Pek Sil Lum / Brian Klingborg and Lai Hung
    p. cm.
  ISBN 0-8048-3164-5 (pbk.)
  1. Kung fu. I. Lai, Hung. II. Title
GV1114.7.K54 1998
796.815'9—dc21   98-48403
                              CIP

Distributed by

USA	JAPAN
Tuttle Publishing	Tuttle Shokai Ltd.
RR 1 Box 231-5	1-21-13, Seki
North Clarendon, VT 05759	Tama-ku, Kawasaki-shi 214
(800) 526-2778	Japan
(800) FAX-TUTL	(044) 833-0225
	(044) 822-0413
SOUTHEAST ASIA	CANADA
Berkeley Books Pte. Ltd.	Raincoast Books
5 Little Road #08-01	8680 Cambie Street
Singapore 536983	Vancouver, Canada V6P 6M9
(65) 280-3320	(604) 323-7100
(65) 280-6290	(604) 323-2600

First edition
05 04 03 02 01 00 99   1 3 5 7 9 10 8 6 4 2
Printed in the United States of America
Book Design by Peter Holm, Sterling Hill Productions

Acknowledgments

Sincere thanks are owed to all those who contributed their time, expertise, and enthusiasm to this book, especially: Sifu Mark Poppendiek of the UC Davis LHCMAI and Sifu Gary Tang of the Richmond LHCMAI—both of whom offered valuable advice on the text, helped with the tortuously complicated photography process, and shared insight and knowledge gained from more than twenty years with Lai Hung; Harriet Lai, for her invaluable help with translation; Michael Henry, for contributing to the photography; Mark V. Wiley, for seeing potential in the initial manuscript and for guiding me along the way; and above all, my wife, Lanchi, for her encouragement, patience, and support, and also for letting me hog the computer!

In my collaboration with Lai Hung, I provided the written words and he provided the martial expertise. Although I have done my utmost to present Lai Hung's considerable knowledge as accurately as possible, any defects or errors contained within the following pages are due solely to my incomplete grasp of his teachings rather than to any imperfections in Lai Hung's mastery of the Pek Sil Lum art.

A Note on the Text

A variety of dialects are spoken in China, two of the most widespread being Mandarin and Cantonese. Since the majority of Chinese martial arts instructors currently teaching in the United States and Europe have their ancestral roots in the province of Kwangtung, they are primarily Cantonese speakers, and as such, Cantonese tends to be the dialect used when referring to martial arts techniques in the Chinese language. Most of the terms in this book, however, are presented in Mandarin, because that is the dialect with which I am most familiar. There are several types of pronunciation guides available for rendering Mandarin into phonetic symbols, but I have chosen to use the Wade-Giles system of Romanization. Notable exceptions to this rule are the name of Lai Hung and the term Pek Sil Lum, both of which are presented in their Cantonese form.

Contents

Introduction 1

Part One: History and Overview
1. What Is Kung-fu? 7
2. A Brief History of the Chinese Martial Arts 9
3. The Origin of Pek Sil Lum 15
4. Sifu Lai Hung 19

Part Two: Theory
5. On Ch'i and Ch'i Kung 29
6. Chinese Medicine and Martial Arts 33
7. The Chinese Martial Arts Code of Ethics 35

Part Three: Pek Sil Lum Basics
8. The Pek Sil Lum Bow 39
9. Stances 41
10. Footwork 47
11. Kicks 51
12. Hand Techniques 59
13. Basic Exercise Routine 67

Part Four: Form and Function
14. Purpose of Forms Training .77
15. Tuan Ta: Pek Sil Lum's Foundation Form 79
16. Applications of Tuan Ta 101

Afterword 119
Lineage of Sifu Lai Hung 123
Glossary 125
Endnotes 128

Introduction

This book is a guide to the theory and practice of the traditional Chinese arts known collectively in the west as kung fu. Our specific topic is the kung fu style Northern Shaolin[1], but much of the history, techniques, and concepts described herein relate to the martial arts as a whole. Hence, regardless of your preferred martial arts style and whether your interest lies in the historical and theoretical aspects of kung fu or purely in its practicality as a form of self defense, we are confident you will find something of value in the following pages.

Bookstores are now filled to overflowing with martial arts manuals. Some of the more popular Chinese styles about which numerous books have been written include Wing Chun, Tai Ch'i Ch'uan, and Hung-gar. Yet, while one or two books on various aspects of Northern Shaolin have already appeared in print, to our knowledge this manuscript represents the first attempt to comprehensively expalin the history, development, and fundamentals of Northern Shaolin, and to place it within its proper context among the pantheon of the Chinese martial arts.

Currently, a vast number of modern schools claim to teach Northern Shaolin, but what they are in fact offering is a stew of various martial arts which may or may not have originated in Northern China or even within the Shaolin temple organization. Genuine Northern Shaolin is a distinct and discrete style with a very specific curriculum. This curriculum will vary from instructor to instructor and may feature a variety of auxiliary forms, but for it to be classified as Northern Shaolin it must include the following ten core forms: Open the Gate, Lead the Way, Astride the Horse, Pierce the Heart, Martial Technique, Short-Distance Fighting, Plum Blossom Moves, Leaping Strides, Linked Moves, and Skilled Method.[2]

In the context of the Chinese arts, Pek Sil Lum is classified as a northern and an external system. All arts that originated north of the Yangtze River are considered northern, examples of which include Shaolin Lohan, Hsing-I, Northern Praying Mantis, and Pa Kua. Those arts from south of the Yangtze, such as Hung-gar, Wing Chun, and Choy Lay Fut, fall under the category of southern styles. A common perception is that southern Chinese styles emphasize low, solid stances and focus on a variety of upper-body and hand techniques, while northern styles are characterized by higher stances and a diversity of kicking skills.

An external style such as Pek Sil Lum is one that relies primarily on strong, forceful techniques requiring a great deal of muscular power. In contrast, an internal style focuses on developing ch'i, an important concept to which we will return in a later section of this book. Ch'i is said to surpass muscular power in its ability to heal, harm, and protect one's body. In reality, however, the division between internal and external is largely exaggerated. It is true that in the beginning stages the Pek Sil Lum practitioner concentrates on learning techniques that require a great deal of endurance, flexibility, coordination, and power. Yet as the practitioner progresses to the more advanced stages, he or she will learn to cultivate and use ch'i.

Pek Sil Lum is especially renowned for its huge repertoire of kicking techniques. These range from simple front kicks to jumping twirling crescent kicks and the impressive tornado kick, which will be featured in a later section of this book. Yet even though Pek Sil Lum has its roots north of the Yangtze River, it does not neglect upper-body techniques. In fact, the ten core forms include a wide assortment of open- and closed-hand strikes, as well as a plethora of hidden seizing and joint-locking maneuvers.

In addition to the ten core forms, the Pek Sil Lum curriculum features a two-person empty-hand sparring form and a number of weapon forms. Weapons taught include the staff, spear, saber, and broadsword, as well as the more exotic double sabers, double-hook swords, nine-section chain whip, three-section staff, long-handled knife, halberd, and various other classical Chinese instruments of war. While some may question the practicality of learning to wield such archaic weapons, the basic skills mastered through this kind of training can easily be applied in the real world. In the hands of a weapons-savvy martial artist, everyday objects such as stools, towels, chains, keys, pens, and so on can become deadly.

The expertise and inspiration for this book are provided by a Pek Sil Lum and Choy Lay Fut expert who has lived and learned the martial arts for an incredible fifty-two years—Sifu Lai Hung **(Fig. 1)**. I first met Lai Hung in 1989 when I joined the UC Davis Kung-fu Club, where he taught the traditional way, with lots of sweat, a little blood, and a great deal of fun. At first sight, Lai Hung scarcely looked like the fierce fighter he was reputed to be—he stood no more than five feet eight inches tall, was of slight build, and, if not groaning over the form of some hapless student, usually displayed a friendly, relaxed smile.

Before taking up Pek Sil Lum with Lai Hung, I had tried my hand at other martial art styles, but I found the ritualized formality of training in many of these schools somewhat overbearing. With Lai Hung I discovered the joy inherent in studying the martial arts. When Lai Hung demonstrates one of the complicated Pek Sil Lum maneuvers, he frequently laughs with childlike glee as he leaps into the air to deliver a jumping kick or spins on the ground to apply a leg sweep. Although the martial arts are a deadly serious endeavor, under Lai Hung's tutelage they are also an exhilarating form of recreation and enjoyment.

Lai Hung and I conceived this book with a dual purpose in mind: first, to provide a basic course of instruction in the fundamental techniques of traditional Pek Sil Lum; and second, to furnish the reader with a factual and sensible overview of the Chinese martial arts as a whole.

The instructional portion of this book introduces skills that every aspiring martial artist must master, including stances, footwork, kicks, and hand techniques. Once this essential groundwork has been established, the reader will learn an exercise routine that, over time, will both hone these basic skills and condition the body. Our course of instruction will culminate in the presentation of an authentic Shaolin form called tuan ta (short-distance fighting). Tuan ta is the most fundamental of the Pek Sil Lum core forms and it teaches basic skills such as striking, blocking, sweeping, grappling, kicking, and how to fight several opponents at once. To our knowledge, tuan ta has never before been made accessible to the general public. The final chapter offers photographic depictions and examples of the practical applications of this form.

In addition to illustrating the purely physical aspects of Pek Sil Lum, the following pages are intended to dispel a few popularly held misconceptions regarding the Chinese fighting systems. We feel this task is especially important because nowadays the vast majority of material concerning the martial arts—Chinese and otherwise—that appears in print, on television, in the cinema, or even in new forms of media such as the Internet consists mainly of hyperbole, hearsay, and nonsense. We are hopeful that our attempts here will encourage a more balanced view of the myriad Chinese martial styles, which are truly so extraordinary that they require no additional embellishment.

PART ONE
HISTORY AND OVERVIEW

Chapter 1
What Is Kung-fu?

In the West, we are accustomed to using the term kung-fu when referring to any Chinese martial art, no matter what the specific style may be. It will surprise some readers to learn, however, that kung-fu is not a synonym for "the Chinese martial arts." Among modern-day Chinese practitioners, these disciplines are known as kuo shu, wu shu, wu kung, and a variety of other appellations—but only rarely as kung-fu.

A literal translation of kung-fu is "the effort and time it takes to accomplish a task or master a skill." Another suitable translation might be "perfection achieved through exertion." In other words, kung-fu is not in itself a skill—such as proficiency in the martial arts—but is rather the process of labor and practice through which a skill or ability is developed. Over the years, kung-fu has become synonymous with the Chinese martial arts because tradition maintains that it requires at least a decade of devoted effort to master any of the Chinese martial styles.

The technically correct term to use when referring to a fighting system is wu shu. Translated directly from the Chinese, *wu* means "military, warlike," and *shu* denotes a "skill or method of doing something." Although wu shu more precisely embodies the meaning of "martial art," the use of kung-fu in this sense is so popular and widespread that the two terms have essentially become interchangeable.

Although history has supposedly witnessed the creation of over 1,500 wu shu styles, only about 150 of these have survived to the present day. While certain basic similarities exist among the various styles, in many respects they are profoundly different from one another. The advantage to this diversity is that a prospective martial artist is able to choose the style that best suits his or her interests and abilities. Currently, some of the more commonly taught styles include Hung-gar, Wing Chun, praying mantis, Choy Lay Fut, White Crane, and t'ai ch'i ch'uan.

Neither kung-fu nor wu shu as described above should be confused with the official wu shu that is practiced in the People's Republic of China. PRC wu shu is primarily a performance art rather than a fighting system. It originated several decades ago when PRC officials realized the value of the

Chinese martial arts as a cultural promotional tool. For political reasons, however, many of the more practical fighting techniques were removed from the traditional styles and what remained was blended with folk dance, Chinese opera, and acrobatics. While this form of wu shu is less martial than the more combat-oriented styles, it is nevertheless kung-fu of the highest order.

Chapter 2
A Brief History of the Chinese Martial Arts

Popular legends trace the origin of the Chinese martial arts to an Indian monk named Bodhidharma. It is said that Bodhidharma was born into India's noble warrior class, the Kshatriya, but that early in life he renounced his worldly position and became a disciple of Mahayana Buddhism. Around A.D. 520, Bodhidharma left India and made his way to China. He was initially warmly received by Emperor Wu-ti, but a dispute with the emperor over Buddhist doctrine eventually compelled him to seek refuge in the Shaolin temple in Honan Province. At the time of his arrival at the temple, the monks who lived there were absorbed in a scholarly exploration of Buddhism. Bodhidharma strongly believed that Buddhism was a philosophy to be experienced, not just read about in musty old books. Rather than participate in such a pedantic community, Bodhidharma took up residence in a nearby cave and spent the following nine years meditating in complete solitude. In time, the Shaolin monks came to refer to him as the "Wall-gazing Brahmin." Eventually, Bodhidharma's dedication and self-discipline impressed the monks and they invited him to share his knowledge. Bodhidharma set out to instruct the monks in his rigorous meditation techniques, which he believed were the key to Buddhist enlightenment. He soon discovered that poor health prevented the monks from meeting the physical challenges of his discipline. In response, he devised a series of exercises to strengthen their bodies and minds; these exercises were later set down in writing as the *I-Chin Ching* (Muscle Rehabilitation Classic). These exercises, passed down and modified by generations of Shaolin monks, are believed by many to be the foundation from which the various Chinese kung-fu styles evolved.

While many elements of the above legend are undoubtedly based on fact, others are most likely apocryphal in nature. Historical evidence does testify to the existence of a Buddhist monk named Bodhidharma who introduced Ch'an Buddhism (Zen in Japanese) into China. In addition, sources indicate that Bodhidharma spent some years at the Shaolin temple, and that he eventually died there. It is impossible to determine, however, whether or not he really was the founding father of Chinese kung-fu. On the one hand, as a member of the Indian Kshatriya class, it is likely that he had received training in some form of Indian yoga or martial arts before his conversion to Buddhism. He may have shared these physical techniques with the Shaolin monks in the form of the *I-Chin Ching*. On the other hand, there is absolutely no concrete evidence to support the claim that Bodhidharma was the author of the *I-Chin Ching*, or that this work gave rise to the Chinese kung-fu styles.

Some scholars believe that basic martial arts techniques were first developed in India and later transported to China along with other elements of Indian culture. The previously mentioned Kshatriya class were known to have practiced some form of unarmed fighting as early as 1000 B.C.[3] It is conceivable that, centuries before Bodhidharma's lifetime, these skills were transmitted along trade routes into China, where they formed the basis for Chinese kung-fu.

The ancient Greeks also popularized a number of fighting styles, some of which made use of kicking, punching, and grappling techniques. Scholars have speculated that in the wake of Alexander the Great's conquest of India in 326 B.C., these techniques were imported into India, and exported from India to China.[4]

Long before Alexander's campaigns, however, the Chinese were practicing large-scale organized warfare. Numerous historical sources, such as Ssu Ma Ch'ien's *Records of the Historian*, tell us of epic battles and martial derring-do dating back to the Chou dynasty (1122–221 B.C.). Judging from these accounts and the ancient arms and armor that have been unearthed by archaeologists, the Chinese were using relatively sophisticated combat techniques even during this early period.

Regardless of whether the inspiration for Chinese kung-fu came from Greece, India, or China itself, there is little doubt that the Shaolin temple evolved into the most influential martial arts center the world has ever known. According to legend, the Shaolin monks did not engage in any martial arts training prior to the arrival of Bodhidharma, but within a scant 150 years of his death they had already earned a reputation as formidable fighters. By A.D. 600, their fighting prowess was so renowned that the founder of the T'ang dynasty (A.D. 618–907) enlisted their support in his bid for the throne.

For a period of one thousand years, beginning with the T'ang dynasty, the Shaolin temple experienced a golden age. Living in relative peace and prosperity, the monks were free to pursue the twin disciplines of Buddhism and kung-fu. It was during this millennium that additional Shaolin temples were constructed, the most famous of which was the southern Shaolin temple, established in Fukien Province around A.D. 1399.

The Fukien temple was supposedly the site of the celebrated thirty-five chambers in which Shaolin disciples learned different Kung-fu techniques. This temple is also said to have featured a corridor containing eighteen wooden dummies, which served as a kind of graduation examination for students who had completed the training program. In order to qualify as a kung-fu master, acolytes had to pass through this corridor without being injured or killed by the mechanically operated dummies. According to legend, those who made it all the way through faced one final challenge: Using only their forearms, they had to lift and carry a heavy iron urn filled with hot coals. One side of the urn featured a relief of a dragon, while the other was inscribed with a tiger. If the acolyte succeeded in lifting the urn, the dragon and tiger emblems were branded onto his forearms, forever marking him as a Shaolin master.

The invasion of the Manchus and the subsequent founding of the Ch'ing dynasty (A.D. 1644–1911) signaled the decline of the Shaolin temple organization. The Manchus, as foreign invaders attempting to assert control over a vast territory of hostile natives, made it a priority to eliminate all possible sources of resistance. They naturally regarded with great suspicion the famous fighting monks of the Shaolin temple organization. In 1736, the Ch'ing emperor ordered an attack on the Fukien Shaolin temple. With the assistance of a traitorous monk, the temple was destroyed and many of the monks killed.

While Ch'ing harassment was undoubtedly unpleasant for the Shaolin monks, in a strange way it ultimately proved beneficial to the growth of the Chinese martial arts. Prior to the Ch'ing dynasty, the practice of Chinese kung-fu was largely restricted to disciples of the Shaolin temple organization. With the destruction of the Fukien temple, however, a number of Shaolin monks fled into the countryside, where, for the first time, they began to teach their arts to ordinary people. Throughout the remainder of the Ch'ing dynasty, Shaolin kung-fu continued to spread outside the confines of the temple walls. In this manner, just as a forest fire sparks the growth of new trees, the persecution of the Shaolin temple organization was the catalyst for the dissemination and renewed growth of Chinese kung-fu during the nineteenth century.

In the waning years of the Ch'ing dynasty, the Shaolin temples were allowed to resume activity without interference, but their importance as the center of Chinese kung-fu continued to diminish into the early years of the twentieth century. In 1911, the imperial government was overthrown, and the country was subsequently divided into territories controlled by various local warlords. Eventually, the Nationalist leader Chiang Kai-shek embarked upon a campaign to strip the warlords of their power and reunify the country under central leadership. This campaign proved to be the final undoing for the Shaolin temple in Honan Province.

In 1927, Chiang dispatched General Feng Yu-hsiang to Honan Province to fight the warlord Fan Chung-hsiu. It so happened that the abbot of the Shaolin temple, Miao Hsing, was a good friend of Warlord Fan. General Feng soon rousted Fan in battle, forcing the latter to take refuge in the Shaolin temple. When Feng arrived to capture Fan, Miao Hsing ordered his monks to attack the government troops in a bid to save the vanquished warlord. In the ensuing skirmish the monks were no match for the guns of Feng's soldiers and many were killed, including Miao Hsing. After the battle, Feng ordered the temple burned to the ground.[5]

Although this was the final straw for the Shaolin temple organization, the study and practice of Chinese kung-fu continued to flourish in the countryside. It was during this period that a number of lay organizations dedicated to the martial arts were founded. The first of these, the Ching Wu Association, was established in Shanghai in 1909.

In 1927, the newly restored Republican government created the Central Kuo Shu Institute in Nanking to consolidate, organize, and promote Chinese kung-fu. The institute brought together five famous martial artists, known to posterity as the Five Tigers of Northern China. One of the Five Northern Tigers was the Pek Sil Lum and ch'i kung expert Ku Ju-chang, whose student Lung Tze-hsiang was later to become Lai Hung's Pek Sil Lum instructor.

A few years later, the Five Northern Tigers went to Canton and established a second institute along with a group of renowned masters known as the Five Tigers of Southern China. One of the Five Southern Tigers was a Choy Lay Fut expert named T'an San, whose pupil Li Ch'ou was later to become Lai Hung's Choy Lay Fut instructor.

In 1937, the Japanese invaded China and the nation spent the next eight years at war. Later, as World War II drew to a close, the Chinese became embroiled in a civil war between the Nationalist government and Communist insurgents. After the Chinese Communists ascended to power in 1949, Chinese kung-fu came to be regarded as an unpleasant relic of the past. Many Chinese martial artists eventually emigrated to Hong Kong, Singapore, and other parts of the world, where they could continue to practice their arts without interference. And so this tradition lives on today.

There is a curious footnote to the story of the Shaolin temple organization. During the kung-fu craze that swept the world in the 1970s and again in the early 1980s, a number of movies featuring heroic Shaolin monks were filmed. Before long, kung-fu fans around the world came to regard the Shaolin temple organization as the ultimate martial arts academy. When China eventually opened its gates to tourism, visitors clamored to see the Honan temple. Unfortunately, by this time the temple had fallen into a state of great disrepair. The Chinese government soon recognized that the temple represented a potential tourist gold mine, and initiated a program to have it refurbished. While there is currently some debate over whether the monks now inhabiting the Shaolin temple in Honan are truly Shaolin disciples or simply kung-fu performers capitalizing on the tourist industry, it is now possible for anyone to pay for instruction at this historic site!

Chapter 3
The Origin of Pek Sil Lum

The roots of Pek Sil Lum are obscure and open to debate. No one knows for sure when the system originated, what styles influenced it, or who exactly was responsible for developing its ten primary forms. Yet without exception, all legitimate Pek Sil Lum instructors today trace their lineage back to one of the twentieth century's most celebrated martial artists: Ku Ju-chang **(Fig. 1)**.

Ku Ju-chang was born in Chiangsu Province around 1894. His father, Ku Lei-chi, owned a business that provided armed escorts for merchants and rich civilians traveling through the bandit-infested roads leading to and from Nanking. Ku Lei-chi apparently had a connection to the Honan Shaolin temple and was himself an accomplished practitioner of the martial art style known as t'an t'ui, which originated within China's small Muslim community. The elder Ku died when Ju-chang was about fourteen years old, but before passing away, he told his son to seek out a Shaolin monk named Yen Chi-wen, who was at that time living in Shantung Province. Two years later, at the age of sixteen, Ku Ju-chang left home to begin his studies with Yen Chi-wen. By most accounts, Ju-chang studied with Yen Chi-wen for eleven years, mastering various Shaolin temple styles. Whether the ten primary forms of Pek Sil Lum were passed on to Ku Ju-chang directly from Yen Chi-wen is impossible to say. It does seem likely, however, that Yen Chi-wen taught Ku Ju-chang the iron palm and ch'i kung techniques that later made him famous throughout China.

Ku Ju-chang had already attained some fame by the late 1920s, when he participated in a martial arts competition sponsored by the National government and the martial arts community. He is said to have finished among the top ten in this competition, which was, by most accounts, the largest and most prestigious ever witnessed in China up to that point. Around the time of this competition, the Nanking Central Kuo Shu Institute was founded, and Ku Ju-chang was invited to serve as one of its martial arts instructors. The institute succeeded in bringing together the preeminent martial artists of the day, known as the Five Tigers of Northern China. This select group included Ku Ju-chang, Wan Lai-sheng, Fu Chen-sung, and Li Hsien-wu. Aspiring martial artists flocked to the institute to take advantage of the opportunity to study with these renowned masters.

A year or so later, these five patriarchs went to Kwangtung Province to assist in the organization of a second Kuo Shu Institute in Kwangchou.

There, they were joined in their endeavors by a group of famous martial artists known as the Five Southern Tigers, most notably among them a Choy Lay Fut practitioner named T'an San **(Fig. 2)**. Ku Ju-chang opened a school not far from T'an San's academy, and these two eventually came to openly exchange both knowledge and students. It seems likely that both T'an San and Ku Ju-chang incorporated techniques learned from the other into their respective styles, perhaps modifying them as a result.

In addition to his exchange with T'an San, Ku Ju-chang is said to have studied a variety of other styles with famous masters, including hsing-i, pa kua, and Sun style t'ai ch'i with Sun Lu T'ang, Wutang sword style with Li Ching-lin, and ch'a fist with Yu Chen-sheng. History, however, best remembers Ku Ju-chang for his iron palm and ch'i kung abilities. Examples of his skill include breaking thirteen stacked bricks with a single silent slap, allowing a car to be parked on his stomach, and so on **(Figs. 3 and 4)**. The

most famous story regarding his prowess is supposed to have occurred in 1931. As legend has it, a circus from a foreign land arrived in Kwangchou with a wild horse as its star attraction. The circus promoter (often said to be a Russian) offered a reward to anyone who could tame the horse. Apparently a number of martial artists tried to subdue the horse and were kicked or trampled. Eventually, however, Ku Ju-chang stepped up and slapped the horse once on the back. The unfortunate

beast died soon after and an autopsy revealed that its internal organs had been severely damaged. This is doubtless a highly romanticized version of what actually happened.

A perhaps more accurate version of the story is that Ku Ju-chang visited the circus with some of his students and asked to see the horse. When the circus promoter realized that Ku Ju-chang was one of China's premier martial artists, he immediately apologized for issuing the challenge and retracted it on the spot. He then took Ku Ju-chang to see the animal. Ku Ju-chang ran his hands across the horse's back and under its belly, commented on the smoothness of its coat, and left without further incident. Several days later a rumor erupted that the horse died soon after of internal bleeding, as a direct result of Ku Ju-chang's iron palm technique.

Ku Ju-chang survived both the Japanese invasion of China and the turmoil that was to follow. He continued to teach Pek Sil Lum until he died in his mid-sixties. He was survived by several students, one of whom was Lung Tze-hsiang. When the Chinese Communists assumed power on the mainland in 1949, Lung Tze-hsiang moved to Hong Kong, where he later taught Lai Hung.

It should be noted that many teachers nowadays use Pek Sil Lum as a general term to denote the mélange of styles and techniques that emerged from the interaction of the Five Northern and Five Southern Tigers during this watershed period in the history of Chinese martial arts. In addition, there is another branch of Pek Sil Lum that was transmitted through Yen Shang-wu, who, along with Lung Tze-hsiang, studied under Ku Ju-chang; this style differs slightly from the one presented here, but, we wish to emphasize, it is by no means less valid or "traditional" **(Fig. 5)**. As a

result, there is currently some variation between the Pek Sil Lum taught from one school to the next. Suffice to say, however, if the school's lineage extends directly back to Ku Ju-chang and features the ten core forms, it is part of the Pek Sil Lum family.

Chapter 4
Sifu Lai Hung

Lai Hung (Fig. 1) was born into troubled times in a troubled country—the year was 1938 and the place was China. At the time of Lai Hung's birth, China had been mired in a desperate struggle against the invading Japanese army for just over thirteen months. In that brief period, the well-equipped and modernized Japanese forces had stormed Beijing, smashed through heavy resistance in Shanghai, and laid waste to Nanking, forcing the Chinese government to beat a hasty retreat to the remote province of Szechwan. The effect of these hostilities on ordinary Chinese citizens was severe—food and other necessities were scarce and violent death was an everyday occurrence.

China's war of attrition against Japan lasted until August 14, 1945, when, in the wake of the bombing of Nagasaki and Hiroshima, the Japanese emperor ordered his nation's forces to lay down their arms. But China's troubles did not end along with the Sino-Japanese War. Immediately after the Japanese surrender and withdrawal from Chinese soil, a civil war broke out between the Nationalist forces under Chiang Kai-shek and the Communists under Mao Tze-tung. This internal struggle raged on for another four years, exacerbating the already intolerable conditions in China.

The hardships faced by the young Lai Hung, who until the age of ten had never known a life in which there was not war and suffering to be endured, no doubt influenced certain aspects of his character. These character traits, shared by many through history who spent their formative years in a similarly harsh environment, included persistence in the face of adversity, determination, self-discipline, and an ability to withstand pain, hunger, and discomfort. Interestingly enough, it is perhaps precisely those traits, born out of the adversity he faced early in his life, that made possible Lai Hung's later achievements in the martial arts arena.

Lai Hung's father worked as a bodyguard and was an avid student of the Chinese martial arts. Having lived through periods of great turmoil himself, the elder Lai believed in the necessity of knowing how to defend oneself. Soon after Lai Hung's eighth birthday, his father arranged for him to commence his martial arts training with a famous master named Lee Nam. Sifu Lee taught a practical and powerful style not unlike Choy Lay Fut known as hung t'ou fo wei. Around this time, Lai Hung also received instruction from two other well-known teachers, one of whom was nicknamed "Master Iron Palm" and the other "the Iron-Headed Mouse."

In 1949, the Lai family emigrated to Hong Kong, where both Lai Hung and his father found work at a shoe manufacturing company. Soon thereafter, Lai Hung sought instruction from the famous teacher Lung Tze-hsiang **(Fig. 2)**. Lung was one of a few senior students who were recognized as legitimate successors to Ku Ju-chang. At the time, the Hong Kong Athletic Association served as an informal headquarters for martial arts instruction and training in Hong Kong, and Sifu Lung's classes were held there. Under Sifu Lung's guidance, Lai Hung embarked upon his study of traditional Pek Sil Lum, classical Chinese weapons, Yang-style t'ai ch'i ch'uan, and various forms of ch'i kung.

Initially, Lai Hung's mother objected to his martial pursuits. Years of poverty and food shortages had left Lai Hung skinny and frail, so naturally his mother was concerned that his training would lead to injury. But within a few months of joining Sifu Lung's class, she noticed dramatic improvements in his posture and overall health. From that time on, she fully encouraged his desire to learn Chinese kung-fu.

In the period immediately following World War II, Hong Kong emerged as a fertile environment for the continued development and expansion of the Chinese martial arts. This was primarily due to the fact that dozens of famous masters from all over China fled to the island territory when the Communists assumed power on the mainland. Young students like Lai Hung benefited enormously from this chain of events. For the first time in history, accomplished practitioners of every conceivable style found themselves living together in a very small, interdependent community. Although this situation produced plenty of conflicts, it also resulted in an unprecedented degree of collaboration between these martial arts patriarchs. As a result, Lai Hung and his fellow pupils enjoyed an unusual amount of interaction with a variety of instructors.

When Lai Hung was seventeen, a famous Choy Lay Fut practitioner by the name of Li Ch'ou was invited to participate in Sifu Lung's classes. Li Ch'ou and Lung Tze-hsiang were actually brothers in the kung-fu lineage—Li Ch'ou was a disciple of T'an San, and in the years when T'an San and Ku Ju-chang were exchanging students, Lung Tze-hsiang had also studied Choy Lay Fut under T'an San. Lai Hung eagerly took advantage of the opportunity to learn this relatively new martial arts style. He soon discovered that he enjoyed the direct simplicity and forcefulness of Choy Lay Fut. Lai Hung continued to study with Li Ch'ou for the next eight years.

Lai Hung's first major martial arts competition was the Hong Kong–Macao–Taiwan tournament held in Taiwan in 1957. At the time, the custom was for Hong Kong's preeminent martial artists, known as the Ten Tigers of Kwangtung,[6] to each select their best students and have them all compete against one another for the honor of participating in important tournaments. Sifu Lung nominated Lai Hung without even bothering to inform the latter of his decision. Lai Hung didn't learn that he was to compete until a few days later, when a group of newspaper reporters showed up at the Athletic Association to interview him.

Lai Hung was unsure of how his father would react to this news, so he kept it a secret. Needless to say, when his father opened up the morning paper several days later and discovered his son's picture and a story on his participation in the upcoming tournament, he was very angry. The elder Lai was concerned that his son would either be injured or would fight badly and cause a loss of face for the family. He initially refused to allow Lai Hung to take part in the competition, but after Sifu Lung invited him to tea and explained the situation, he grudgingly gave his consent. The elder Lai, however, was not content to leave anything to chance, and so he arranged for an old Choy Lay Fut master named Ch'en Chen to come to his house every evening to provide special training for Lai Hung.

In retrospect, the elder Lai needn't have been so concerned. Of the dozens of competitors who fought for the privilege of representing Hong Kong at the upcoming tournament, only Lai Hung and two others made the final cut. These three young men then spent the remaining weeks before the tournament living and training intensively together at the Athletic Association. As the sole representatives for the entire Hong Kong martial arts community, Lai Hung and his friends were under enormous pressure to perform well.

In those early days there were no tournament divisions—fighters were matched against one another regardless of weight, martial art style, school affiliation, or years of training. The tournament fighting lasted several days, during which a number of contestants were seriously injured, as fighters only wore thin, fingerless gloves rather than proper boxing gloves. Among the competitors faced by Lai Hung were regional favorites with elaborate nicknames such as "Thunderfoot" and "King of the Kickers." Lai Hung faced four fighters and beat them all, one with a backfist strike that ripped his opponent's cheek from ear to nose. Although he was the tournament's youngest competitor, just nineteen at the time, he emerged as undefeated grand champion.

Lai Hung returned to Hong Kong a celebrity. He was featured in magazine and newspaper articles and was even asked to appear in a few Hong Kong kung-fu films. But Lai Hung soon discovered that while fame had its advantages, it also had its drawbacks. For one thing, it didn't put food on the table. He still had to work long hours to make ends meet, and also find time to continue his training. In addition, in the Wild West atmosphere of the Hong Kong martial arts community, he was now the fighter everyone wanted to beat. Although Lai Hung always tried to avoid street fighting, on a few occasions he was forced to defend himself against young toughs who were hoping to become famous at his expense. In one exchange, he and one other compatriot defeated a group of six opponents in a rooftop brawl.

Unlike many athletes who lose their competitive edge after their first taste of success, Lai Hung continued to train as hard as ever. He studied Pek Sil Lum with Sifu Lung on Monday and Wednesday evenings and Choy Lay Fut with Sifu Li on Tuesdays and Thursdays. In addition to these formal classes, he followed a regular program of jogging, skipping rope, punching and kicking a heavy bag, and sparring with fellow students. During this period, he was so eager in his training and such a fierce fighter that he earned the nickname "Sang Tze," which, loosely translated, means "Wild Boy."

Lai Hung also sought to improve his skills by learning from other teachers, one of whom was a Pek Sil Lum and hsing-i master named Yeh Yu-t'ing. Sifu Yeh was a former student of the famous master Huo Yuan-chia. The latter was responsible for establishing the original Ching Wu Association in Shanghai in the early 1900s. As a young man, Sifu Huo defeated a number of prominent foreign martial artists. When he subsequently died of poisoning, an event dramatized in the Bruce Lee movie *The Chinese Connection*, it was widely assumed that his assassination had been engineered by Japanese militarists.

A famous fighter in his own right, Sifu Yeh was notoriously picky about who he chose to teach. Nevertheless, having heard many stories about Sifu Yeh's great skill, Lai Hung and four other students went to see him. Of the five young men, only Lai Hung was accepted as a pupil. Not long after Lai Hung began training with Sifu Yeh, a couple of Yeh's older students decided to try out this young upstart. They attacked Lai Hung one day during class and were fairly well pummeled for their trouble. Even though they came out on the short end of the exchange, Sifu Yeh yelled at them for picking a fight with a fellow student and forced them to apologize for their rude behavior.

In 1961, Lai Hung was selected to compete in a tournament to be held in Thailand. This tournament was his first experience with the muay Thai style of kickboxing. In addition to facing a completely new style of fighting, Lai Hung found himself competing against professional Thai boxers, as they are known, who trained and fought for a living. Even despite these odds, he discovered that he was an equal match for his opponents. Unfortunately, as a result of a misunderstanding, he ended up forfeiting one of his bouts. It seems that during this bout his opponent managed to knock him down. When he regained his footing, the referee inquired in English if Lai Hung wanted to give up the fight. Lai Hung, who at the time spoke no English, thought that he was being asked if he wanted to continue the bout. When he responded by nodding his head enthusiastically, the referee declared him the loser.

Disappointing as it was to lose in this way, Lai Hung found the Thailand tournament a valuable experience. He was intrigued by muay Thai and eventually added many of its techniques to his more traditional fighting style. In addition, he adopted Western boxing techniques gleaned from watching Joe Louis fight on television. In fact, he eventually became so adept at Western boxing that the Taiwanese government asked him to try out for their boxing teams for both the 1962 Asia Olympics and the 1964 World Olympics.

Between 1961 and 1969, Lai Hung competed in five additional tournaments—two in Taiwan, one in Singapore, one in Malaysia, and one in Cambodia. He emerged the undefeated victor in all but the last, when he again faced professional kickboxers. This time his opponents included the number one and number two ranked Southeast Asian kickboxing champions. Lai Hung won his match against the number two ranked champion, but then faced a final bout against the kickboxer ranked number one. In this final bout, he was injured during a particularly savage exchange with his opponent. The champion threw a kick that Lai Hung evaded; Lai Hung then hooked the champion's leg, intending to sweep him, but the champion took Lai Hung by surprise with an upward thrust of his knee. Lai Hung caught the blow directly on his jaw and several of his teeth were shattered. When the final bell rang, Lai Hung accepted the judges' decision in favor of his opponent with good grace and a very sore jaw **(Figs. 3–5)**.

  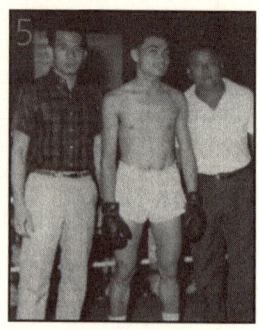

Lai Hung formally established himself as an instructor when still very young by opening the Lai Hung Chinese Martial Arts Institute in Hong Kong in 1962. Students flocked to his classes and in time he produced a number of champion fighters. Lai Hung took his duties as a teacher very seriously. In addition to showing his students the more physical aspects of the martial arts, he also made an effort to provide moral guidance. He never allowed his students to engage in street fighting or to bully others, and he disciplined or expelled those who behaved inappropriately. He always encouraged his students to contribute to an orderly and peaceful society. On one memorable occasion, Lai Hung and his students took to the streets to help restore order and prevent looting when Hong Kong experienced a series of riots in 1967.

There are a number of anecdotes about Lai Hung that shed additional light on his personality. On one occasion, he was walking down a street in Kowloon when he felt a pickpocket reach into his pants and grab his wallet. Rather than harming the pickpocket, Lai Hung simply applied a wrist lock and escorted him several blocks to the local police station, where he turned him in. Years later, soon after emigrating to the United States, a church organization in Oakland asked him to hold classes at one of their facilities to discourage the gang activities that were taking place there. After Lai Hung and his students began practicing at the facility, a few gang members asked to participate. Lai Hung told them they were welcome to join—as long as they followed the moral precepts required of all Shaolin students.

Some gang members did join the classes, but Lai Hung eventually had to expel them for misbehavior. Naturally, they took offense, and as Lai Hung left the facility after class one evening, he found a dozen armed gang members waiting for him. Rather than allow matters to escalate, Lai Hung suggested that the leader of the gang come see him for a chat. A few days later, Lai Hung and the gang leader had a conversation at a Chinatown restaurant that ended with the leader formally apologizing for his compatriots' rudeness and promising to ensure that the gang caused no more trouble at the church's facilities.

In 1971, Lai Hung visited the United States for the first time. While staying in San Francisco, he received a telephone call from Bruce Lee, who was then working on a movie script in Los Angeles. Lai Hung had come to know Bruce through a fellow student of Sifu Lung's with whom Lee's father studied t'ai ch'i ch'uan. In addition to this connection, Lai Hung was acquainted with Bruce in another context. For many years a rivalry had existed between Choy Lay Fut and Wing Chun students in Hong Kong. On one or two occasions some of Lai Hung's more rambunctious students had quarreled with Bruce, who was associated with the Wing Chun school. As he strongly disapproved of this kind of activity, Lai Hung immediately intervened whenever these conflicts arose. Of course, Bruce was also familiar with Lai Hung's reputation as a full-contact fighter and patriarch of the Pek Sil Lum and Choy Lay Fut schools. During their phone conversation, Bruce politely encouraged Lai Hung to open a studio in California so that, as Bruce put it, "I will have a suitable place to train." Like millions of others around the world, Lai Hung was shocked and saddened to hear of Bruce Lee's death in 1973.

Soon after his arrival in the United States, Lai Hung was invited to serve as a martial arts instructor at the San Pablo Police Department. In 1972, Lai Hung opened a branch of the Lai Hung Chinese Martial Arts Institute on Columbus Street in San Francisco. He has since taught Pek Sil Lum and Choy Lay Fut in Oakland, San Jose, Berkeley, Richmond, Davis, and Sacramento, California. Over the past twenty-five years, he has trained hundreds of students, many of whom have competed successfully in international tournaments. The Lai Hung Chinese Martial Arts Institute currently maintains branches in Sacramento, Davis, Richmond, and New York. In addition to his duties as head instructor of the LHCMAI, Lai Hung serves as director of the United States Pek Hsing Choy Lay Fut Association, and in 1996 was acknowledged by a congress of Choy Lay Fut elders as the head of the international Pek Hsing Choy Lay Fut family.

PART TWO
THEORY

Chapter 5
On Ch'i and Ch'i Kung

Ch'i and ch'i kung are concepts that, half-shrouded in legend and often the subject of exaggeration, are poorly understood by most martial arts practitioners. There are numerous written accounts and word-of-mouth tales regarding kung-fu masters who had the ability to extinguish a candle from across the room simply by pointing at it, or who could knock an assailant backward without even making physical contact. With stories such as these, it is no easy task to separate fact from fiction when it comes to ch'i and ch'i kung. In this chapter I will try to provide a more balanced view of these important concepts.

Ch'i is usually translated as "vital energy" or "life force." One way to think of ch'i is as the fuel that powers our physical existence. All living things possess ch'i, and when ch'i is absent, death results. The Chinese character for ch'i depicts steam or vapor rising from cooked rice. Interpreting this character, we see that ch'i is an immaterial and intangible substance, like steam, which is the distilled essence of a material substance, such as rice. Thus, one way to conceptualize ch'i is as the energy our bodies produce by absorbing nutrients from the things we eat. We eat rice, absorb its nutrients, and this provides fuel for our physical growth and movement. Ch'i, however, is not only the distilled essence of a material substance. It is also an invisible force through which the material world takes shape. For example, while rice is a material substance from which we absorb ch'i, the growth of rice is in turn fueled by the ch'i it absorbs from its environment. So, in the broadest sense, ch'i is the force that generates and animates life and all the processes of life.

In the past ten years, a number of Western scientists have researched ch'i and many are now convinced that it does indeed have a basis in fact. A current hypothesis contends that ch'i is an electromagnetic field that generates and maintains living organisms. In this respect, ch'i is not unlike a car battery—it is a source of power that flows throughout the body, providing energy for all the necessary physical functions. It is interesting to note that many Chinese manuals on the cultivation of ch'i insist that the practitioner should align himself with the earth's magnetic fields while performing ch'i kung exercises.

Ch'i kung is the practice of cultivating and regulating one's ch'i through breathing, movement, and meditation exercises. The benefits of ch'i kung are said to range from the prevention and cure of illness to the alleviation of chronic disorders of the digestive, respiratory, cardiovascular, and nervous systems. The basic theory underlying ch'i kung is that ch'i circulates in the body through specific channels just as blood circulates through a network of veins and arteries. When the circulation of ch'i is blocked or out of balance, a physical or psychological problem can result. By restoring the smooth and balanced circulation of ch'i, these problems will disappear.

The importance of ch'i, in the context of martial arts, is that it is the foundation of internal power. Although one's muscular strength can be increased through physical training such as weight lifting, there are limits as to what the muscles can accomplish. Internal power, gained through manipulation of ch'i, is said to surpass physical power in its ability to harm, heal, and protect the body. Internal styles of martial arts, such as hsing-i, pa kua, and t'ai ch'i emphasize the development of ch'i over purely physical techniques. External styles of kung-fu, including Pek Sil Lum, for example, first emphasize external techniques and later move on to the cultivation and manipulation of ch'i.

Lai Hung believes that, at its most basic level, what martial artists call ch'i is really just a product of breath control and proper physical and mental technique. Take, for example, a martial artist who can perform seemingly incredible feats such as breaking bricks with his bare hands or absorbing heavy blows to the body. The average spectator, who does not have these abilities, may believe the martial artist to possess superhuman powers. In fact, such feats are not unlike hitting a home run in Yankee Stadium. While hitting a home run may be impossible for an ordinary person, a professional baseball player who trains specifically for this purpose every day is able to do so with some regularity. In other words, the extraordinary abilities attributed to ch'i are often simply the result of training, technique, and talent, rather than any kind of mysterious or supernatural power.

Although a kung-fu practitioner who has mastered proper technique and control can develop some amazing abilities, he is still subject to the same physical laws as the rest of us. An accomplished martial artist can withstand a physical attack that may cause serious injury to an ordinary person, yet this does not mean that he is invincible. No matter how adept one is at manipulating ch'i and using physical technique, a properly executed knife thrust or bullet from a gun will still result in injury and death.

This is not to say that all the amazing stories about ch'i are necessarily false. As previously mentioned, some scientists have likened ch'i to an electromagnetic field. In their conception, ch'i is like electricity—a form of energy that can produce light, heat, magnetism, and chemical changes. Interestingly enough, many ch'i kung masters are reputed to have the ability to produce heat, light, and even sparks from their fingertips. If ch'i is truly a kind of electricity, then such claims are indeed within the realm of possibility. Until science can determine the exact properties of ch'i, it is best to keep an open, yet rational, mind in these matters.

Lai Hung maintains that one of the reasons the martial arts should be studied under a qualified instructor is because ch'i cultivation can be very harmful to the body if done incorrectly or in too short a period of time. If a student learns too quickly, without taking the time to ensure the proper flow of ch'i through his body, he will cause himself serious internal injuries. Lai Hung describes this syndrome as pao cha, which literally means "to explode."

Although Lai Hung studied iron palm and ch'i kung techniques with Lung Tze-hsiang, he is quick to point out that there is nothing supernatural about these skills. Regardless of how well one has mastered ch'i kung, the best policy is always to avoid getting hit or kicked. Lai Hung does encourage his students to focus on what he considers to be the most basic form of ch'i manipulation: breath control. When sinking into a stance, one should exhale; when rising up or executing an expansive movement, one should inhale. Lai Hung also emphasizes a form of biofeedback in which students learn to control their breathing by monitoring their pulse rate.

Chapter 6
Chinese Medicine and Martial Arts

As a pursuit based on the techniques of physical combat, Chinese kung-fu is bound to result in occasional injuries among its practitioners. For this reason, martial artists were traditionally taught to heal as well as to harm. Training in this respect usually emphasized skills such as bone-setting, acupressure/acupuncture, and herbal medicine. Many kung-fu masters still practice a combination of acupressure/acupuncture, herbology, and ch'i kung as a means to regulate their bodies and maintain good health.

The basic theory underlying the science of acupuncture is related to the flow of ch'i through the body. Ch'i circulates through various channels in the body, known as meridians, regulating our physical processes. When the circulation of ch'i becomes blocked or unbalanced in some manner, illness is the result. Ch'i can be physically manipulated at specific points along the meridian system. These spots are known as gates or cavities, of which there are believed to be between seven hundred and eight hundred. Acupuncture and acupressure are essentially the practice of pressing or inserting needles into these gates, respectively, in order to restore the proper flow and balance of ch'i in the body.

The other side of the coin is that a martial artist can cause harm by striking or manipulating ch'i gates. This is the essence of the skill known as *tien hsueh*, or "attacking vital points." In the martial arts arsenal there are 108 gates that can be used in this manner. Of these gates, 72 produce local paralysis or fainting, while the remaining 36 can cause death.

Recent research confirms that acupuncture and acupressure techniques are effective, but scientists are still unsure exactly why and how they work. One theory is that acupuncture blocks the transmission of pain signals along the nervous system to the brain and simultaneously promotes the release of the body's own natural painkillers. Another theory asserts that acupuncture serves as a kind of control panel for regulating ch'i, which in turn regulates our various physical processes.[7]

Herbal medicine is often used hand-in-hand with acupressure and acupuncture techniques. Chinese herbologists claim not only that their remedies are as effective as Western pharmaceutical drugs, but that they are superior in two respects. First, Western drugs are excellent for treating specific physiological symptoms, but they do not address the underlying problem or imbalance that causes the symptoms. For example, drugs may eliminate the symptoms of a cold, but they do not improve a person's resistance to catching colds. Second, while Western drugs do eliminate specific symptoms, they also often have unwanted side effects. Chinese herbs, on the other hand, contain a blend of several natural substances that not only treat a specific malady but also counteract such side effects. In addition, herbs can be ingested regularly to keep bodily functions in balance and to prevent the onset of illness or disease.[8]

While in Hong Kong, Lai Hung undertook a special course of study in traditional Chinese medicine and is certified in this field. He believes that traditional medicine and martial arts are inseparable and should always be studied together. To this end, he has in the past sponsored scholarly exchanges in the United States with faculty from Chinese medical schools overseas.

As a result of his training in Chinese medicine and his experience as a fighter, Lai Hung has some interesting theories regarding what foods one should avoid. For example, he never eats duck because he believes it impedes the body's natural healing process. In addition, he maintains that eating sticky rice will exacerbate inflammation of injured joints and turnips harm the respiratory system. Lai Hung also does not smoke or drink. He does not criticize others for drinking in moderation, but he believes someone who is training seriously should avoid drinking—otherwise their competitive edge will be blunted and they will be unable to completely devote themselves to their training regimen.

Like many traditional martial artists, Lai Hung has spent years developing a formula consisting of various herbs and other natural ingredients for an ointment designed to treat ligament and muscle injuries. If massaged into the injured joint or muscle, this ointment will reduce swelling and bruising, as well as promote improved circulation and more rapid healing.

Chapter 7
The Chinese Martial Arts Code of Ethics

As the evolution of the Chinese martial arts was intimately connected to the development of Ch'an Buddhism, it is not surprising that traditional kung-fu was concerned with ethical, as well as physical, cultivation. Many teachers still maintain, perhaps somewhat naively, that only the virtuous can truly achieve mastery of the martial arts. Nevertheless, while there is certainly no shortage of kung-fu schools where the instructors and students engage in thuggish behavior, for the most part the martial code of ethics has survived intact. The following is a set of basic standards Lai Hung requires of his students:

Ten Rules Students Must Follow
- Respect teachers and elders
- Respect fellow students
- Help the weak and endangered
- Be resolute in your goals
- Follow a regular work and rest schedule
- Do not be covetous or licentious
- Do not lie or accuse falsely
- Do not lose your temper or harbor hatred
- Do not harm living creatures
- Do not disturb the peace

PART THREE
PEK SIL LUM BASICS

Chapter 8
The Pek Sil Lum Bow

The Chinese traditionally exchange bows as both a form of greeting and a sign of respect. While many modern Chinese have now adopted the Western custom of shaking hands, in the realm of martial arts, where tradition is held sacred, bowing is still the proper way to acknowledge your teacher and fellow students.

Each individual martial arts school has its own variation of the kung-fu bow. Yet most versions of the bow share a common feature: a closed right fist held against an open left hand. Legend holds that this bow originated during the Ch'ing dynasty, when it served as a secret identification signal for patriotic Chinese involved in the struggle to overthrow the foreign Manchu rulers and reinstate the Ming dynasty. In this context, the closed right fist is meant to symbolize the Chinese character for sun while the open left hand represents the character for moon. When these two characters are combined, they form the character for the word Ming, from which the Ming dynasty derived its name.

The following is the formal bow specific to Pek Sil Lum. To begin, stand with your feet together and your arms held loosely at your sides **(Fig. 1)**. Curl your right hand into a fist, straighten your left hand so that the fingers are rigid and held tightly together, and tuck the left thumb into the palm **(Fig. 2)**.

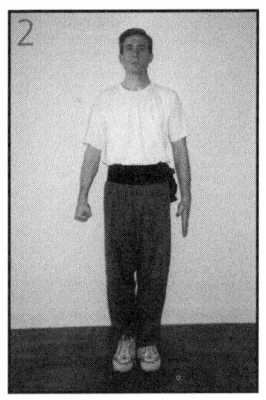

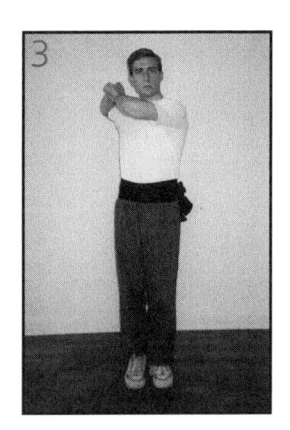

Next, pull your right arm up so that your fist is beside your right ear. At the same time, swing your left hand across your body so that it meets your right hand. Notice that both arms are held parallel to the ground **(Fig. 3)**. Lift your right foot slightly, then simultaneously stamp the ground with your right foot while extending the left leg forward. All your weight should rest on your right leg. Point the toes of your left foot downward and allow them to rest very lightly on the ground **(Fig. 4)**.

Push your right fist and open left hand straight out from your ear to about chest level. Extend both arms as far as you can while still keeping both elbows slightly bent **(Fig. 5)**.

Notice the position of the hands: the space where the first two fingers of the left hand meet the palm sits directly on top of the knuckle of the right index finger. The entire bow should be performed in one smooth, continuous motion.

Chapter 9

Stances

Proper execution of stances is the most basic of martial arts skills. Just as one first learns to crawl before one can run, you must master stances before moving on to more complicated techniques. An often used but appropriate analogy is that a stance is akin to the foundation of a building. As long as its foundation is firm and solid, a building will remain stable and upright. A building with a weak foundation is easily toppled.

The function of a stance is threefold: to protect vulnerable areas of the body; to maintain balance; and to generate power. With regard to the first function, you will notice, as you practice the following stances, that the position of the lower body is always calculated to protect the groin from attack. This is extremely important as victory in more than a few fights has been achieved with just a single well-placed kick to the groin. Knees are another region of vulnerability, especially if they are held locked and rigid. Most Pek Sil Lum stances require the knees to remain bent in order to absorb potentially damaging blows.

Although ground grappling is the bread and butter of many martial art styles, such as the currently fashionable Brazilian jujitsu, Pek Sil Lum is not one of them. In most cases, falling to the ground is the least desirable thing that could happen to a Pek Sil Lum fighter. This is why maintaining balance, especially in the face of attack from a grappling or ground-fighting stylist, is so vital. Strong stances will enable you to remain upright even when your opponent is trying to sweep you off your feet.

The Chinese martial arts rely more on technique, timing, and efficient use of the entire body than on pure strength or brute force. Stances are helpful in this respect because they serve to unite the combined weight and momentum of the body behind the application of each technique. For example, imagine you reach out and strike an object without moving any part of your body other than your arm. Now imagine you twist your upper body and waist in concert with your arm as you strike the object. The second strike, which combines the force generated by the movement of your body with the strength of your arm, will be much more powerful than the first strike. Stances are designed to generate power from the entire body. As a result, they enable a person to kick or punch with as much or more force than a heavier and stronger opponent. Following are the basic stances of Pek Sil Lum.

Ready Position

Stand with your feet together, hands loosely at your sides, your back straight, and eyes forward.

Square Horse (Ssu P'ing Ma)

From the ready position, draw your hands to your waist and wrap them tightly around your middle, pressing lightly on your abdomen with the fingers of each hand **(Fig. 1)**. When first learning the stances, the pressure of your hands on your abdomen will help you to focus on controlling your breath and maintaining a straight posture as you sink into a low stance. When actually performing the Pek Sil Lum forms, you will not place your hands around your waist in this manner.

Place both feet parallel to one another and beyond shoulder width **(Fig. 2)**. Unlike many Chinese styles, especially southern ones, Pek Sil Lum does not usually require the practitioner to widen his stance by shifting his feet outward step-by-step. It is faster to just simply slide your feet to the proper position in preparation for sinking into a square horse stance.

Bend both knees and sink down so that your thighs are almost parallel to the ground **(Fig. 3)**. Exhale as you sink down. Your back should remain straight. Make sure that you are not leaning forward or backward and are not arching the small of your back. Your knees should be positioned over your toes and your feet should remain parallel to one another.

This is an extremely strong, stable stance. It is nearly impossible to sweep, push over, or topple someone who has really mastered the square horse. Another feature of the square horse stance is that it serves to protect the vital areas—especially the groin. From the square horse it is also possible to rapidly shift into any of the other major stances in preparation for attack or defense.

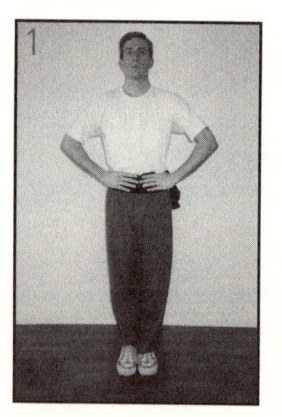

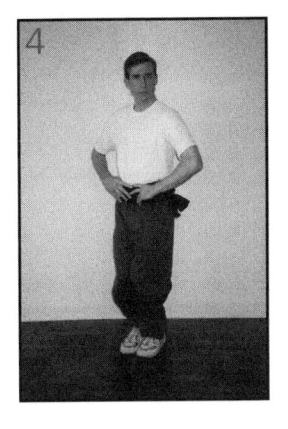

Bow Stance (Ch'ien Kung Hou Chin)

Start from the ready position with your hands wrapped around your waist and your fingers pressing lightly on your abdomen. Bend your knees while keeping your back straight, then twist your knees and hips slightly to the right **(Fig. 4)**. Following this, extend your left foot directly forward and plant it firmly on the ground with the toes pointing inward **(Fig. 5)**. Your back leg remains straight with the right foot firmly planted. The toes of the right foot will point forward. Your hips will also point directly forward, rather than off to the side or at a forty-five-degree angle. As with the square horse, make sure that your back is perfectly straight and that you are not leaning forward, backward, or to either side. If you are performing the bow stance correctly, your left knee will be positioned directly over the toes of your left foot **(Fig. 6)**. In fact, if you look down, you will notice that your left knee is blocking your view of the left foot.

Like the square horse, this stance is very stable and serves to protect the groin. Many of your forward attacking techniques will be executed while in the bow stance, so it is vital to learn how to perform it correctly.

Rearing Horse (Tiao T'i Ma)

Start from the ready position with your hands wrapped around your waist and your fingers pressing lightly on your abdomen. Bend your knees, look to your left, and extend your left foot **(Fig. 7)**. The toes of your left foot should be pointed downward and curled in slightly toward the center of your body. Your left knee should be angled inward slightly to protect the groin **(Fig. 8)**. Keep all your weight centered on your right leg. In fact, you should just barely touch the ground with your left foot. Your right foot should point slightly to the left (the direction of your extended foot). When this stance is used in a combat situation, you extend your leg in the direction of your opponent.

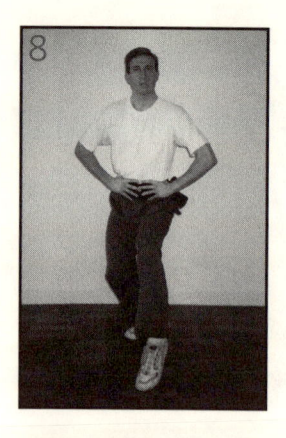

The rearing horse stance, called a cat stance in many other styles, is a versatile attack or defense posture. From this position, you can easily shift into other stances or move in virtually any direction. Since no weight is placed on the extended leg it is not vulnerable to sweeps and can quickly be chambered in preparation for a kick or to defend against an opponent's kick. In the footwork section of this book, we will demonstrate how a rearing horse can be applied in a takedown technique.

Golden Chicken (Chin Chi Tu Li)

Start from the ready position with your hands wrapped around your waist and your fingers pressing lightly on your abdomen. Lift your left leg straight up so that your thigh is parallel to the ground **(Fig. 9)**. Your toes should be pointed downward and slightly angled in toward the center of your body **(Fig. 10)**. This foot position serves to tighten the muscles in the front of your shin so that they protect your shinbone against the impact of a strike. In actual practice, this posture serves to protect the groin or leg from a low kick. If your opponent is attacking with a low roundhouse kick, you may want to angle your knee out to the side slightly so that you take the impact of the kick on your thigh or the outside of your shin. Be careful not to angle your leg to far to the side, as this will leave your groin unprotected.

Rooted Stance (Cha T'ui)

Start from the ready position with your hands wrapped around your waist and your fingers pressing lightly on your abdomen. Place your feet slightly wider than your shoulders, as when performing a square horse stance. Bend your right knee while keeping your left leg straight and sink down into a crouch **(Fig. 11)**. Keep your upper body and hips pointed toward the left foot. Keep your back as straight as possible. Your feet should be parallel to one another and flat on the ground.

This stance is excellent not only for avoiding an attack but also for launching a counterattack. For example, if your opponent lashes out with a high attack, simply sink down into a rooted stance to avoid being struck. Before your opponent can reset himself for a renewed attack, spring up from the rooted stance with a forward punch or a jumping front kick.

This is a difficult stance for beginners, so don't expect to get it right on the first try. With time and increased flexibility, you will be able to master the rooted stance.

Twisting Horse (Niu Ma)

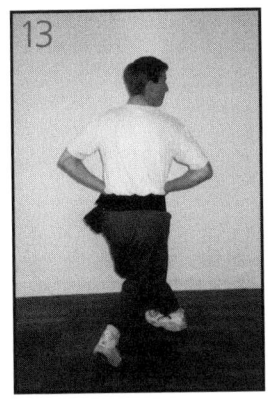

Begin this from a square horse stance. Turn your head and look to the left **(Fig. 12)**. Now twist your upper body, followed by your waist and lower body, 180 degrees to the left **(Fig. 13)**. Your chest will now be pointing in the opposite direction of where you started. You will, however, continue to look toward what was originally your left, since this is where your opponent is located. When you turn to the left, pivot on your left heel and right toe, and vice versa when you turn to the right. When executing a left twisting horse, your left leg is in front and your right leg is bent so that the knee lightly touches your left calf. Your left foot remains flat on the ground while the right heel is lifted. In practice, this stance is usually used when turning the body 180 degrees in preparation for a footwork maneuver (as in the square horse/sliding horse routine presented below) or when delivering a kick with the rear leg. In order to execute a rapid sliding horse or rear leg kick after having shifted into a twisting horse, almost no weight should be placed on the rear leg.

Below is a reference chart to help you to remember the fundamentals of each stance:

Stance	Weight Distribution	Right Leg	Left Leg	Hip Direction	Feet
Square Horse	Even	Slightly wider than shoulder width, thigh almost parallel to ground	Slightly wider than shoulder width, thigh almost parallel to ground	Forward	Parallel to each other toes facing forward
Bow Stance (left side)	60% forward (left) leg, 40% rear (right) leg	Completely straight	Bent with knee directly over toes	Forward	Left foot pointed inward, right foot forward
Rearing Horse (left side)	0% left leg, 100% right leg	Knee bent, supporting weight	Extended, knee bent	Facing in the direction of the extended leg or at a 45 degree angle to to the right of the extended leg	Right foot pointing toward left, left foot pointing down with toes curled inward
Golden Chicken (left side)	0% left leg, 100% right leg	Completely straight, supporting weight	Knee bent, thigh parallel to ground	Forward	Left foot pointing down, right foot pointing forward
Rooted (left side)	90% right leg, 10% left leg	Knee fully bent	Leg straight, extended	Facing left (direction of extended leg)	Both feet flat on ground, parallel, facing forward
Twisted Horse (left side)	90% front (left) leg, 10% rear (right) leg	Knee bent, lightly touching back of left calf	Knee bent	Facing backward (from original position)	Left leg flat on ground, right heel off gound

Chapter 10
Footwork

The following routines are essential for developing proper footwork. In the same way that stances are equivalent to "crawling," these basic footwork movements are the "first steps" you will take on your way to mastering Pek Sil Lum. Without proper footwork, you will forever lack the ability to maintain stability and generate power in your techniques.

As a long-range fighting style, Pek Sil Lum relies on the ability to rapidly close the distance on an opponent for a fast attack and to retreat just as quickly out of harm's way. The three footwork routines presented here will familiarize you with the mechanics of shifting from stance to stance without losing your balance and, as a result, your ability to deliver powerful offensive and defensive moves when facing an opponent. Each routine should be practiced until you can perform it smoothly, quickly, and without sacrificing form and stability in your stances.

Routine #1: Square Horse to Sliding Horse

Step 1: Begin this routine in the square horse stance **(Fig. 1)**. ***Step 2:*** Look to your left and retract your left foot to shift into a left-facing rearing horse stance **(Fig. 2)**. ***Step 3***: With all your weight on your right leg, retract your left foot until it is almost touching your right foot **(Fig. 3)**. ***Step 4***: Thrust out your left foot to propel your entire body to the left several feet **(Fig. 4)**. Both feet

The Secrets of Northern Shaolin Kung-Fu

should slide across the floor rather than hopping up off the ground. End in a square horse stance **(Fig. 5)**.

Step 5: Look to your right and repeat these same movements to the right side. Continue to slide to the left and to the right, without pausing, for ten to twenty repetitions.

The sliding horse maneuver has several fighting applications. First, a sliding horse is a simple means for moving quickly toward an opponent for an attack. Second, it can be used to unbalance or destabilize the stance or posture of an opponent. For example, if your opponent is in a modified bow or fighting stance with his left leg forward, use this technique to slide in behind his forward leg, applying sudden force with your left thigh to the underside of his thigh. If you direct your force upward and backward, you will uproot his stance. Similarly, if your opponent is to your left with his left leg forward, slide into his stance so that your left leg is behind his left leg. Then, using your left leg as a pivot, simply hook your arm around his body and push him backward over your leg. This, however, is only advisable if you can prevent him from hitting you as you slide in to execute the takedown maneuver.

Routine #2: Square Horse to Twisting Horse to Sliding Horse

Step 1: Begin this routine in the square horse stance **(Fig. 6)**. Look to the left. ***Step 2***: Twist your body 180 degrees to the left to shift into a twisting horse stance **(Fig. 7)**. Notice that you are now looking over your right shoulder (in the direction of your opponent). ***Step 3***: Leading with your right (rear) foot, slide in the direction you are looking **(Fig. 8)**. End in a square horse stance. ***Step 4***: Look to the left **(Fig. 9)**. Repeat these moves to return to your original position.

Step 5: Repeat the steps in the opposite direction. Continue this sequence of movements to either side for ten to twenty repetitions.

This is similar to the sliding horse routine above, except that this maneuver allows you to turn your stance around so that you can slide the proper leg behind your opponent in preparation for a takedown move. In addition, this is an excellent method of moving in a lateral direction while maintaining a protective posture and firm footing.

Routine #3: Link Stances

Step 1: Begin this routine in the square horse stance **(Fig. 10)**. ***Step 2***: Look to your left. Retract your left leg to shift into a left-facing rearing horse stance **(Fig. 11)**. ***Step 3***: While still looking to your left, lift your left leg to form a golden chicken stance **(Fig. 12)**. ***Step 4***: Extend your left leg and sink down into a rooted stance **(Fig. 13)**. ***Step 5***: Transfer 60 percent of your weight to your left leg and stand up into a left bow stance **(Fig. 14)**. ***Step 6***: Shift back to a horse stance facing front.

Step 7: Repeat these movements to the right. Continue this sequence of movements for ten to

twenty repetitions.

This general routine will teach you how to shift from stance to stance while maintaining proper balance and posture. Concentrate on forming a strong, stable stance with each shift. When performing this sequence of movements, inhale as you rise up and exhale as you sink down.

Chapter 11
Kicks

A common perception is that the Chinese martial arts that originated in the south emphasize low, solid stances and focus on upper-body techniques, whereas the northern arts are characterized by higher stances and a variety of kicking skills. The accepted wisdom is that the south is a region of crowded cities and countless waterways, leading southern martial artists to develop styles suited for use on the slippery decks of boats and in bustling marketplaces. While it is true that in many respects the idea that northern styles are more kick-oriented, there are countless exceptions. For example, the renowned Wong Fei-hung, a practitioner of Hung-gar, which, along with Wing Chun, is perhaps the most popular southern style, was famous for his "no-shadow" kicking techniques. In addition, hsing-i, a style that history traces back to practitioners from the northern provinces of Shansi and Honan, includes very few kicks.

In keeping with this perception, Pek Sil Lum is indeed a style that features a variety of energetic, leaping kicks. Pek Sil Lum is primarily a long-range fighting system—a martial artist from this style avoids the close in-fighting characterized especially by Wing Chun—and kicks are used both offensively and defensively to prevent an opponent from getting close enough to cause harm.

There are an almost infinite variety of kicks, but not all are suited to an actual combat situation, whether it be in the ring or on the street. Lai Hung eschews the spinning back kicks and other fancy maneuvers that are the bread and butter of many popular martial arts styles. Such moves require the kicker to turn his back on his opponent as he winds up to unload a leg attack—a fast fighter can use this brief window of opportunity to step in behind the kicker, simultaneously jamming the kick and delivering a counterattack. This is a technique Lai Hung used effectively on many occasions. Even a slower martial artist, if he knows how to read the signs that his opponent is about to deliver one of these moves, can simply back out of range before the kicker can complete the attack.

Most of the kicks featured in Pek Sil Lum forms are very direct, either straight ahead front kicks, side kicks, or jumping front kicks. These are the techniques that tend to be the most effective in fighting situations as they are fast and powerful. The more advanced forms, however, do include a wide variety of acrobatic kicking techniques such as spinning kicks, combination kicks, and so on.

Heel Kick (Teng T'ui)

Step 1: Begin this kicking technique from the ready position, with your hands around your waist and your fingers pressing lightly against your abdomen. Step forward with your left leg **(Fig. 1)**. ***Step 2***: Bring your right knee up so that it is higher than your waist **(Fig. 2)**. ***Step 3***: Thrust your foot straight out from its elevated position with your toes pointing up and back **(Fig. 3)**.

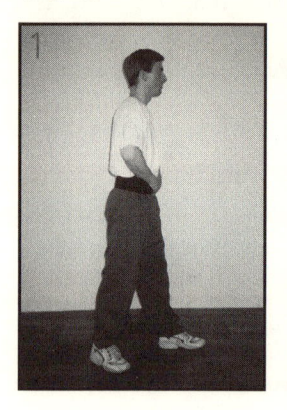

The striking surface of this kick is the heel of your foot. Many styles prefer to curl the toes backward and use the ball of the foot as the striking surface. Pek Sil Lum doesn't make much use of this type of kick, but either the heel kick or the following toe kick can be modified to use the ball of the foot if the individual practitioner so desires.

When practicing the heel kick, use an open space in which you can walk back and forth. Start with the right heel kick, as explained above. When you have completed your right heel kick, simply drop your right leg down and step forward on your right foot. As you step forward, lift your left knee, kick, and then drop your left leg down and step forward on your left foot as you chamber your right leg in preparation for a right heel kick. Continue to step, chamber, and kick in this manner. Focus on keeping your back straight and thrusting your foot out, rather than kicking upward. Concentrate on kicking to your front center and in the same spot with each kick.

This is a versatile kick. You can use it as a frontal attack by simply stepping toward your opponent and kicking. Since the power in the heel kick comes from thrusting straight outward, it is best to limit your target area to below chest level, rather than trying to kick too high. Another use for this kick is to jam the forward motion of an oncoming opponent. This works especially well if your opponent is rushing toward you with a punching attack and is not adequately guarding his groin or abdomen. Since the motion of a heel kick is so simple, this is also one of the fastest and most practical kicking techniques you can use.

Lai Hung often uses a variation of this kick in which he sinks down on his supporting leg by bending his knee slightly as he delivers the kick. The sinking motion serves to increase the body weight and force behind the technique. This type of kick is especially effective for striking at the lower leg or knee of an opponent. Lai Hung's favorite target for a direct front kick, however, is just above the groin in the pit of the stomach. Striking opponents here can not only cause them to double over in immense pain but can cause very serious internal injuries as well.

Toe Kick (T'i T'ui)

Step 1: Begin this kicking technique from the ready position, with your hands around your waist and your fingers pressing lightly against your abdomen. Step forward with your left leg **(Fig. 4)**. *Step 2*: Bring your right knee up so that it is higher than your waist **(Fig. 5)**. *Step 3*: Kick your foot outward with an upward snapping motion. Keep your toes pointed forward **(Fig. 6)**.

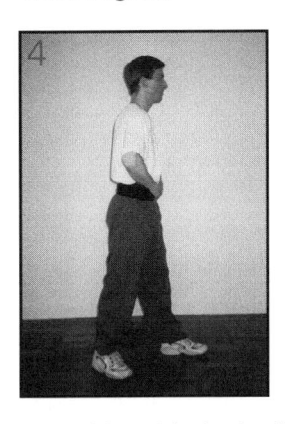

Unlike with the heel kick, you actually want the force of this kick to swing upward from the chambered position, in a quick, snapping motion, rather than straight outward. The preferred striking surface of this kick is the shin.

When practicing the toe kick, use an open space in which you can walk back and forth. Start with the right toe kick, as explained above. When you have completed your right toe kick, simply drop your right leg down and step forward on your right foot. As you step forward, lift your left knee, kick, and then drop your left leg down and step forward on your left foot as you chamber your right leg. Continue to kick, step, chamber, and kick in this manner. Focus on keeping your back straight and allowing the force of your kick to swing upward in a quick snapping motion. As with the heel kick, concentrate on kicking to your front center and in the same spot with each kick.

This kick can be used to attack the groin, sternum, or throat, but in an actual combat situation it is usually converted into a roundhouse kick directed at the head, ribs, or legs. In such a case, the kicking leg is chambered and then hooked up, inward, and down toward the target. The real power in this technique stems from snapping the leg fluidly like a whip as the hips and torso are turned in the direction of the kick to produce momentum and force.

A roundhouse kick can be used in both long and short ranges. In a long-range situation, the instep of the foot is usually the striking surface, whereas at a short range you will use your shin to strike your opponent, or, if you are very close, perhaps even use your knee to deliver the blow. Practically speaking, a roundhouse kick is most effective when directed at a low target, such as the thigh or floating ribs. High kicks are flashy and exciting, but they require the kicker to chamber in an elevated position before lashing out with the kick. Not only is this more time consuming than striking with a simple roundhouse kick to an opponent's thigh, but the high chamber position will immediately reveal one's intention to kick high, thus giving an experienced opponent an opportunity to devise the perfect counter. In addition, the foot and ankle are very delicate mechanisms, and striking a target with the instep can often cause foot and ankle injuries.

Outside Crescent Kick (Wai Pai Lien T'ui)
Step 1: Begin this kicking technique from the ready position, with both hands held at chest level **(Fig. 7)**. *Step 2*: Step forward and at an angle slightly to the left with your left foot **(Fig. 8)**. *Step 3*: Without bending your knee, swing your right leg all the way to the left, and then up to head level, and across to the right in one continuous, circular motion **(Fig. 9)**. Slap your left and right hands with your foot as it travels across your body. The striking surface of this kick is the outside edge or heel of your foot.

This kick doubles as both a block and an attack. As it is very powerful, it is sometimes effective for jamming an opponent's fierce forward attack, although such a maneuver could potentially leave you off-balance and open for a counterattack. Also, an outside crescent kick is often used as a counter against a knife attack. In such a case, the kick should be directed at the wrist, forearm, or elbow of the arm holding the knife to either injure the arm, cause the attacker to drop the knife, or simply push the arm holding the knife out of the way to create an opening for a counterattack.

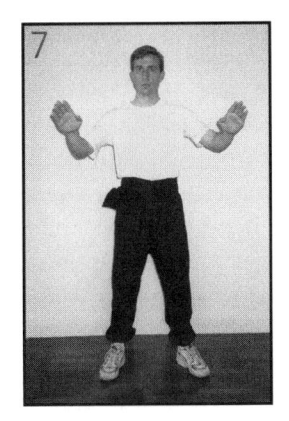

Inside Crescent Kick (Nei Pai Lien T'ui)

Step 1: Begin this kicking technique from the ready position, with both hands held at chest level **(Fig. 10)**. *Step 2*: Step forward and at an angle slightly to the left with your left foot **(Fig. 11)**. *Step 3*: Without bending your knee, swing your right leg up to the right side, across your body at head level, across to the left, and finally back down to the right in one continuous, circular motion **(Fig. 12)**. Slap your left hand with your foot as it travels across your body. The striking surface of this kick is the inside edge or heel of your foot.

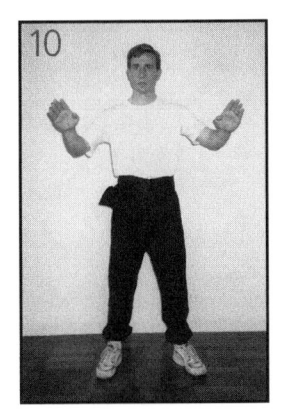

An inside crescent kick is often used as part of a block-and-counter combination. If your opponent kicks at you with his right leg, swing your right leg in an inside crescent kick to strike the inside of his leg, thus blocking the kick. Without dropping your leg, shift your hips to the left and thrust in toward your opponent's groin, inner thigh, or abdomen with a low side kick.

Double Jumping Kick (Shuang Fei T'ui)

Step 1: Begin this kicking technique from the ready position, with both hands held out to either side of your body **(Fig. 13)**. ***Step 2***: Lift your right knee until it is parallel to your waist **(Fig. 14)**. ***Step 3***: Bend your left knee and sink down **(Fig. 15)**. ***Step 4***: Cock your right leg to the rear. Leap into the air as you simultaneously thrust your right knee up toward your chest and swing your arms upward to cross in front of your chest **(Fig. 16)**. The upward momentum created by your knee and arm movement will help propel you off the ground. ***Step 5***: While in midair, kick forward with your left foot while simultaneously thrusting both arms down to either side **(Fig. 17)**. ***Step 6***: Land on your right leg, with your left leg forward in a rearing horse stance.

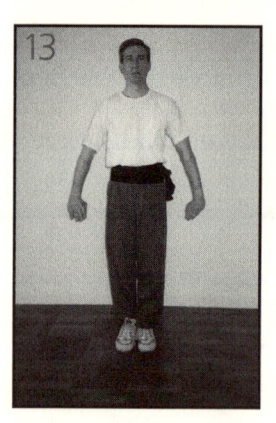

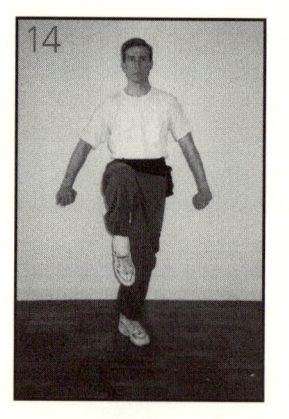

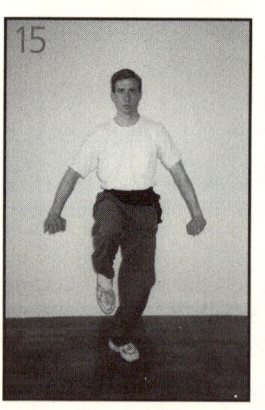

This is a powerful forward attack. The double leg movement coordinated with the arm motion serves to generate momentum for a strong kick. In most cases, you want to direct your attack at your opponent's chest or sternum. A common mistake among beginners is to kick upward, rather than forward, so focus on directing the force of your attack in a straight line to your opponent. This is an effective technique to counter an oncoming attack from an opponent who is larger and stronger than you.

Tornado Kick (Hsun Feng T'ui)

Step 1: Begin this kicking technique from the square horse stance **(Fig. 18)**. ***Step 2***: Swing your arms and upper body to the right in a relaxed manner **(Fig. 19)**. ***Step 3***: Allow your arms and upper body to swing naturally back to the left, slightly lifting your left leg as you do so **(Fig. 20)**. ***Step 4***: Simultaneously, jump straight up and allow leftward momentum generated by your upper body to swing you around 180 degrees. As you swing around, bring your right leg up into an inside crescent kick **(Figs. 21 and 22)**. If you began this exercise facing north, you will be kicking to the south. Slap your right foot into your left hand as it travels across your body. ***Step 5***: Continue to revolve in midair until you are facing the direction from which you started. Land in a solid square horse stance.

If you were to attack someone with this kick, the striking surface would be the inside heel or edge of the foot with which you are performing the kick. This is not the most practical technique in the Pek Sil Lum arsenal; however, it is effective for springing a sudden attack on an opponent to the rear. In addition, the swinging motion of your arms as you wind up for the kick can double as a strike to opponents on either side.

Chapter 12
Hand Techniques

A plethora of hand techniques are used in the Chinese martial arts. Certain techniques and hand positions are specific to a particular style—take praying mantis, for example, which is easily recognizable by the unique way the practitioner holds his hands with the index and middle fingers extended. Similarly, in the drunken style of kung-fu, the practitioner tucks his bottom three fingers into his palm and creates a circle with his thumb and index finger as if he were holding a tiny Chinese wine cup.

Most Chinese styles, however, share a common set of hand techniques. Some of these were supposedly derived from watching how animals fight, and hence have exotic names such as tiger claw, crane beak, monkey paw, eagle claw, leopard fist, and so on. Others, including hook hand and knife hand, are named according to their defensive or offensive function.

Pek Sil Lum favors a more basic set of hand techniques over the more peculiar hand postures featured in various other Chinese styles. The most important Pek Sil Lum techniques are described below.

Fist (Ch'uan)
Begin forming this fist from an open hand **(Fig. 1)**. When your hand is open, always keep your thumb tucked in toward the center of the palm to avoid having it broken when delivering a blow. Curl your fingers inward until they meet the top of your palm **(Fig. 2)**. Curl the upper half of your

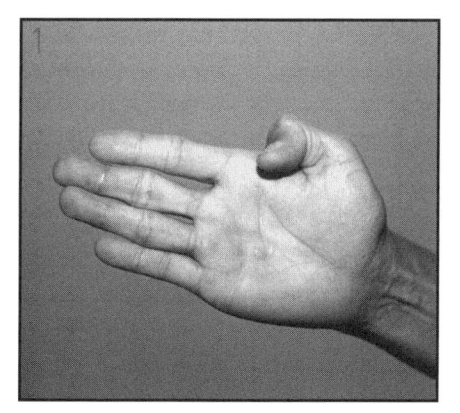

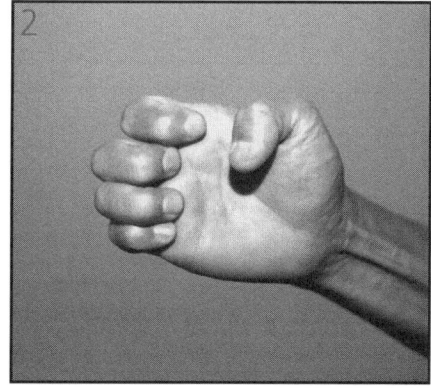

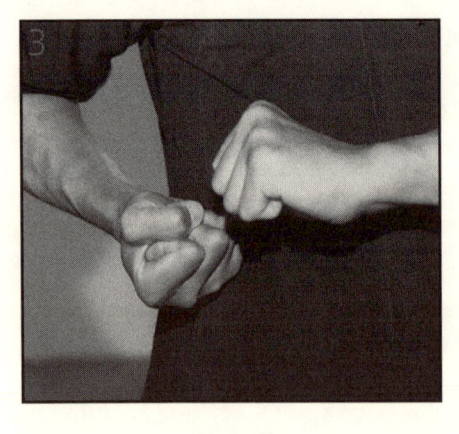

hand inward. Your fingertips should press tightly into your palm and against one another. Place your thumb securely against your fingers **(Fig. 3)**. Notice that the thumb does not rest on top of the fist or protrude out over the second knuckle.

The striking surface of the fist includes the knuckles, the back of the fist (with the striking surface focusing on the crest of the first two knuckles), and the bottom of the fist (in a hammer fist strike).

Some martial arts utilize a method in which the thumb lies on top of the fist rather than alongside the curled fingers. We don't advocate this posture because of the risk of having the thumb broken when delivering a punch. In addition, when the thumb is laid across the curled fingers, as in the Pek Sil Lum version of the fist position, it adds as an extra brace to make the fist tighter—and a tighter fist makes for a more forceful punch.

Vertical Fist (Jih Ch'uan)

In the vertical fist posture, the fist is held upright **(Fig. 4)**. As opposed to other arts that concentrate mainly on horizontal punching techniques, Pek Sil Lum makes extensive use of the vertical fist. In Chinese, this is called a "sun character" fist because it resembles the written character for sun.

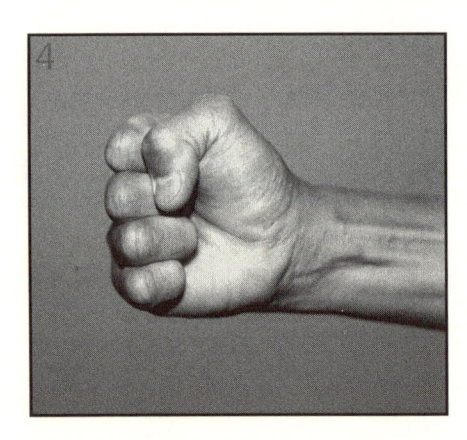

The martial arts community has long debated the virtues of a vertical fist versus a horizontal fist. Each has its relative advantages. Some consider the vertical fist to be slightly more physiologically sound than a horizontal fist. Holding the fist upright allows the impact of a strike to be evenly distributed throughout the bones, ligaments, and cartilage of the wrist and forearm. When the fist is turned sideways, as with a horizontal punch, the fist must be held just so in relation to the wrist and forearm, otherwise the impact will be off-center, thus potentially causing harm to the delicate mechanism of the wrist. A further disadvantage of the horizontal fist is that it requires the elbow of the striking arm to be turned out to the side, leaving it vulnerable to joint locking techniques. If one's arm is captured in this position, it would require only about twenty pounds of accurately applied pressure to dislocate or break the elbow joint. Also, when the elbow is turned outward in this manner, the ribs are left exposed for a counterstrike.

In theory, the vertical fist can be more quickly executed than a horizontal fist simply because it is a more direct technique that does not require one to twist or corkscrew the wrist just before the moment of impact. Some martial artists reason that since speed is a factor in creating power (speed × mass = power), the vertical fist is an altogether more powerful attacking tool.

Horizontal Fist (P'ing Ch'uan)

In the horizontal fist posture, the fist is turned on its side so that the knuckles are at the top **(Fig. 5)**. When executing a horizontal punch, the wrist is turned inward just before the moment of impact to add more force to the strike.

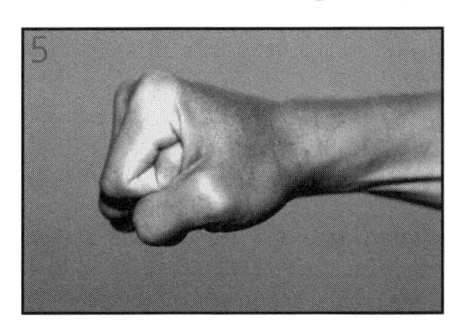

Exponents of the horizontal fist maintain that it provides for a much more powerful strike than the vertical fist, even taking into account that the vertical fist is a slightly faster technique. The rapid turning or corkscrew motion of the wrist that occurs at the moment just before impact provides a bit of extra torque, and this, in turn, adds power to the punch. Another reason why this type of strike is thought by some to be more powerful than a vertical fist strike is that the point of impact is more concentrated. In many Chinese styles, the vertical fist is delivered with the bottom half of the fist; as a result, the impact is spread out over the bottom three fingers or knuckles. A horizontal fist primarily utilizes just the first two knuckles—thus a greater amount of force is delivered over a smaller area of impact, theoretically combining for a more effective penetrating strike.

With regard to its defensive properties, if your opponent grabs your wrist as you deliver a horizontal punch, it is possible to dislodge his grip by quickly reversing the twisting motion of your wrist as you retract your hand.

Fist Ready Positions (Pao Ch'uan)

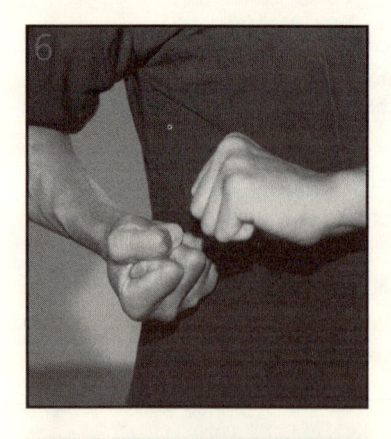

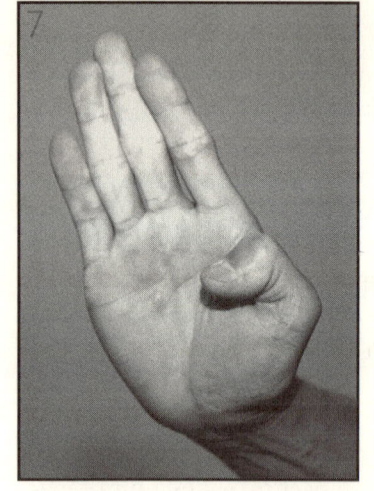

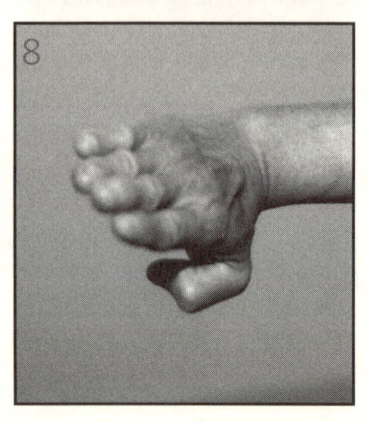

In traditional Pek Sil Lum, before and after executing a hand movement, the fists are chambered at the waist, either with each fist resting atop the hipbones or with both fists together on one or the other side **(Fig. 6)**. Chambering the fists in this manner has several advantages. First, since your hands are resting near the center of your body, you can quickly bring your hands up, drop them down, or bring them across your body to deflect a sudden attack. Second, by keeping your hands close to your body in this manner, you can avoid giving your opponent an opportunity to apply a surprise wrist or arm lock. Third, chambering your fist serves much the same purpose as chambering your leg before a kick. The chambering motion allows you to gather your energy at a central point from which it is then launched in coordination with the movement and momentum of the entire body—especially the waist, hips, and legs.

Palm (Chang)

To deliver a palm technique, hold the hand open with the fingers tightly pressed against one another and the thumb tucked inward toward the palm (to avoid being broken when a strike or block is executed) **(Fig. 7)**.

Striking surfaces for this technique include the fingertips, the heel of the palm, and either edge of the hand. This is an excellent hand position for attacking vital points such as the throat, collarbones, underarms, and sternum, or for manipulating pressure points.

Sometimes the palm is called a knife hand (*shou tao*), especially when it is turned flat **(Fig. 8)**.

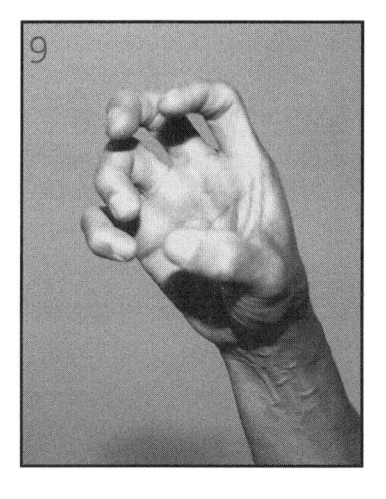

Tiger Claw (Hu Chao)

A tiger claw technique features an open hand with the fingers curled tightly inward **(Fig. 9)**. A tiger claw can be used as an open-handed block, as demonstrated in the form application portion of this book. In addition, a tiger claw can be used to grab someone in preparation for a joint locking technique or a throw, or the fingers can be raked across an opponent's skin in a clawing motion. This hand posture is also suitable for attacking the eyes or face of an opponent. Many southern styles of Chinese martial arts utilize a tiger claw in which the fingers are curled in more tightly and the heel of the palm is used as a striking surface.

Crane Beak (Ho Tsui)

In the crane beak technique, the wrist is bent and the fingers are held tightly together **(Fig. 10)**. Striking surfaces include the fingertips, the top of the wrist, and the back of the hand. When using a crane beak strike or block, you should keep your hand relaxed until just before the moment of impact. Like the twisting motion of a horizontal punch, this allows you to generate extra speed and momentum for a more powerful delivery of the blow. When used as a strike, the crane beak is often turned on its side so that the fingers point toward the middle of your torso rather than toward the ground.

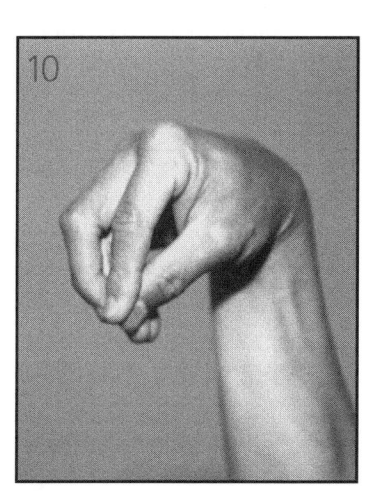

In addition to striking, a crane beak is useful for stripping away an opponent's grip on your wrist or arm. To apply a crane beak for this purpose, simply place the beak on your arm with the heel of the palm resting atop your biceps and the fingers draping down the outside of your arm. Then draw the beak down your arm in a rapid sliding motion to strike your opponent's grip as you simultaneously sink down to pull your wrist free.

Backfist/Roundhouse Strike (Kua Shou Ch'ui)

Step 1: Begin this technique in a square horse stance with both hands chambered on the right side of your body **(Fig. 11)**. *Step 2*: Swing your left arm in a backfist strike to the left **(Fig. 12)**. *Step 3*: As you swing your left arm, turn your hips and torso to the left to provide extra momentum for the strike. As your left hand reaches the target area, allow the motion of your torso turning to the left to naturally propel your right arm in the same direction as your left. Execute a roundhouse strike with your right hand aimed at the same target area as your left backfist **(Fig. 13)**. Your left hand will continue to swing until it comes to a rest behind you. *Step 4*: Chamber your hands on the left side of your body to execute this technique to the right.

The backfist strike with which you initiate this effective combination can serve either as a simple backfist attack to an opponent's head, or as a means to strike away or trap an opponent's guard in preparation for the following roundhouse strike. The roundhouse strike should be directed at your opponent's temple, jaw, or cheek.

Pek Sil Lum is a style that is based on the principles of loose, flowing movement and generating power through momentum rather than brute force. When executing this combination, picture your hands as rocks or pieces of iron and your arms as ropes. Allow your arms to be propelled in a loose, natural motion by the turning of your torso, hips, and waist. Allow your hands to simply follow the flowing motion of your arms.

Cleaving Block/Strike (P'i Ch'uan)

Step 1: Begin this technique in a square horse stance with both hands chambered on your right side **(Fig. 14)**. *Step 2*: Execute a backfist/roundhouse strike to the left **(Fig. 15)**. *Step 3*: Once you have twisted your hips and waist fully to the left side, chamber your right arm slightly and allow the momentum of your body to naturally turn you back around to the right side. As you turn, bring your right arm across in a backfist strike to the right side **(Fig. 16)**. As your right hand reaches the target area, allow the motion of your torso turning to the right to naturally propel your left arm in the same direction as your right.

In a variation of the backfist/roundhouse strike, bring your left arm across your body in a blocking or striking motion with the fist held upright as shown **(Fig. 17)**. This maneuver allows you to either block an incoming strike with your forearm or to apply a strike to your opponent's head with the bottom of your fist. As you bring your left arm across to apply the cleaving block/strike, your right arm continues its natural swinging motion until it comes to rest behind you.

Step 4: Once you have twisted your hips and waist fully to the right side after executing the cleaving block/strike, chamber your left arm slightly and allow the momentum of your body to turn you back around to the left side. As you turn, bring your left arm across in a backfist strike to the left side. As your left hand reaches the target area, allow the motion of your torso turning to the left to naturally propel your right arm in the same direction as your left. In a mirror image of step three, bring your right arm across your body in a cleaving block/strike as your left arm continues to swing behind you **(Fig. 18)**.

When executed rapidly, this combination can serve to simultaneously attack and defend against opponents on either side of you. It is, however, of the utmost importance to coordinate the swinging of the arms and hands with the turning of your torso and waist. It is the turning motion that provides momentum and power for your strikes and blocks.

The cleaving block/strike maneuver can also be used as a joint-locking or -breaking technique. Envision a scenario in which you are squaring off against an opponent with your left foot forward. If he steps in with his left foot in preparation for a strike with his left hand, convert the backfist motion into a grab with your left hand to his wrist. Once you have a grip on his wrist, twist it in a counterclockwise motion to lock his elbow. Next, step around with your right foot and bring your right arm across in a cleaving block/strike technique so that your forearm is applied to the back of his locked elbow. Now, simply press down on his elbow as you continue to apply pressure on his wrist. Your opponent will have no choice but to go down on his knees. Alternatively, you can step around while you have his wrist in your grip and smash your forearm against his locked elbow to break it.

Chapter 13
Basic Exercise Routine

Like the footwork routines presented earlier, the following exercises will help you practice the basic skills necessary for mastering Pek Sil Lum kung-fu. These exercises should be practiced in one continuous flow without pausing and should take between ten to twenty minutes to complete. Once you feel comfortable with the exercise routine and no longer find it strenuous, increase the number of repetitions for each individual section. In addition to providing you with a firm grounding in Pek Sil Lum basics, this routine will increase your strength and endurance, improve your flexibility, and promote the circulation of ch'i throughout your body.

Step 1: Begin this exercise routine in the ready position with your feet together, hands at your sides, your back straight, and your eyes looking forward **(Fig. 1)**. **Step 2**: In a relaxed manner, drag your hands up your sides to your chest, inhaling as you do so **(Fig. 2)**. **Step 3**: Exhale as you push your hands out to either side. Straighten your hands so that your fingertips point upward. Keep your thumbs tucked in toward your palms. Inhale as you push outward with your hands, actively stretching your arms and shoulders **(Fig. 3)**. Exhale and relax your arms and shoulders. Continue to inhale and push outward with your arms, then exhale and relax your arms and shoulders ten to twenty times.

Step 4: Lift your arms above your head **(Fig. 4)**. Form a fist by curling

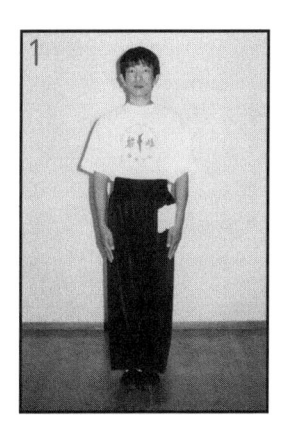

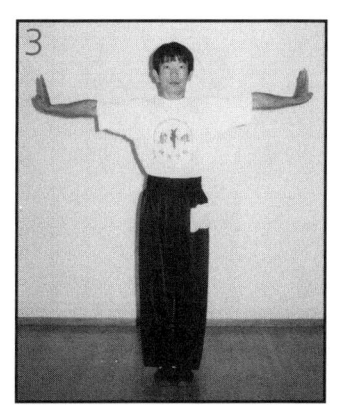

The Secrets of Northern Shaolin Kung-Fu

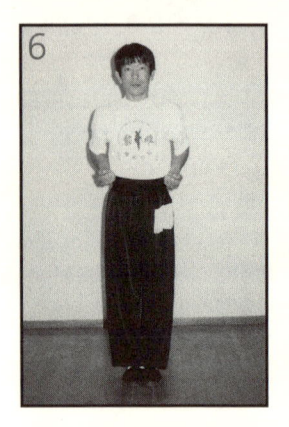

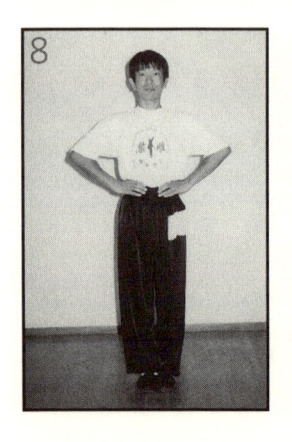

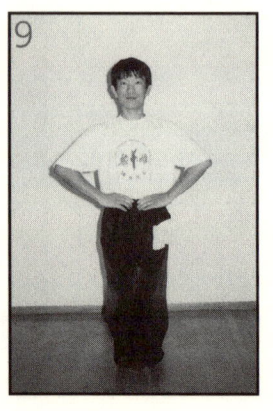

your fingertips inward and wrapping your thumbs securely over your fingers **(Fig. 5)**. Make sure your thumbs don't protrude beyond the second knuckle of your fingers. ***Step 5***: Pull your hands straight down to your waist, inhaling as you do so **(Fig. 6)**. ***Step 6***: Punch forward with a vertical fist while exhaling. Retract your hands to your waist and then punch forward again **(Fig. 7)**. Repeat this sequence of movements ten to twenty times.

Step 7: Drop your arms to your sides, inhale deeply, and then exhale deeply. Resume the ready position with your hands wrapped tightly around your waist and your fingertips lightly pressing on your abdomen **(Fig. 8)**. ***Step 8***: Bend your knees and sink down **(Fig. 9)**. Drop your hands to your sides. Rotate your arms forward, up, and behind you in a flowing, circular motion without straining your muscles **(Figs. 10 and 11)**. Rotate your arms in this manner ten to twenty times.

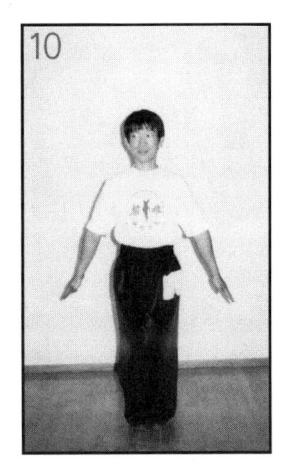

Step 9: Drop your arms to your sides and stand up. Inhale deeply and exhale deeply. Wrap your hands around your waist with your fingers pressing on your abdomen. ***Step 10***: Pivot on your heels so that your toes point forty-five degrees to either side. Raise yourself up on your tiptoes **(Fig. 12)**. ***Step 11***: Sink down into a squat while exhaling **(Fig. 13)**. Keep your back straight and your eyes forward. Raise yourself up on your tiptoes again, and then sink down into a squat. You may have difficulty maintaining your balance at first, but concentrate on keeping your weight centered. Repeat this sequence of movements ten to twenty times.

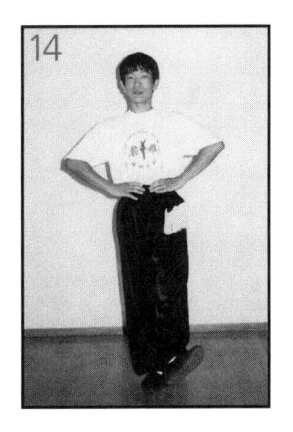

Step 12: Stand up and bring your toes inward so that your feet are together. Extend your left foot forward about five inches off the ground. Rotate your foot in both directions to loosen the ankle **(Fig. 14)**. Repeat this sequence with your right foot. ***Step 13***: Loosen your neck by tilting your head forward, so that your chin meets your chest, and then backward **(Figs. 15 and 16)**. Repeat this sequence of movements ten to twenty times.

Tilt your head to the left until it is almost touch-

The Secrets of Northern Shaolin Kung-Fu

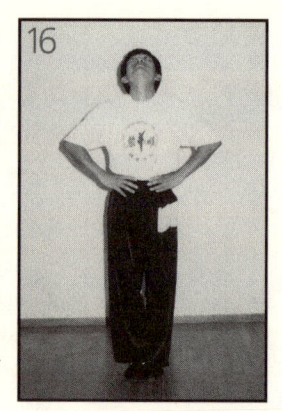

Tilt your head to the left until it is almost touching your left shoulder, and then tilt your head to the right in a similar manner **(Figs. 17 and 18)**. Repeat this sequence of movements ten to twenty times.

Following this, rotate your head in a circle to the left ten to twenty times, then rotate it to the right ten to twenty times. Finally, turn your head rapidly to the left and to the right ten to twenty times **(Fig. 19)**.

Step 14: Bend both knees and turn your hips slightly to the right. Then step forward into left bow stance **(Fig. 20)**. Check the positioning of your feet, legs, and hips. Hold this pose for at least thirty seconds.

Step 15: Stand up as you turn your torso to the right. ***Step 16***: Sink down into a square horse **(Fig. 21)**. Check your posture. Remain in a square horse stance for at least thirty seconds.

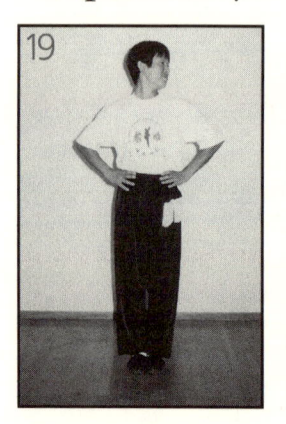

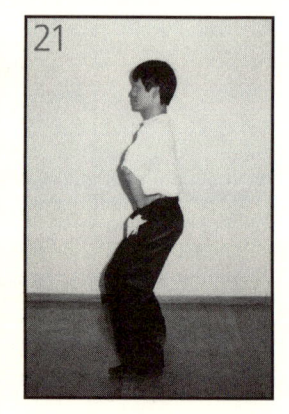

Step 17: Twist your upper body from side to side **(Figs. 22 and 23)**. Be

sure to keep your legs, hips, and head perfectly still during this exercise. Keep your hands near your waist. Repeat this twisting motion ten to twenty times.

Step 18: Retract your left leg slightly and then step forward into left bow stance again. ***Step 19***: Drop your right arm to your side **(Fig. 24)**. Rotate your arm forward, up, and behind you for ten to twenty revolutions **(Fig. 25)**.

Step 20: Retract your left leg and stand up. Inhale deeply and then exhale deeply. ***Step 21***: Bend both knees and turn your hips slightly to the left. Step forward into a right bow stance. Check your posture. Hold this pose for at least thirty seconds.

Step 22: Repeat steps 15 to 19 on the opposite side.

Step 23: Retract your right leg and stand up. Inhale deeply and then exhale deeply. ***Step 24***: Bend both knees and extend your left leg in a left-facing rearing horse stance **(Fig. 26)**. Hold this pose for thirty seconds.

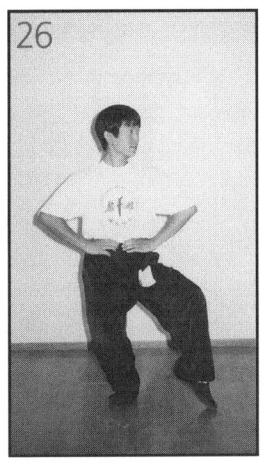

Step 25: Retract your left leg so that is almost touches your right heel and then propel your body to the left several feet, leading with your left foot (this is the sliding horse maneuver). Allow both feet to slide along the ground rather than hopping up off the ground. End this series of movements in a square horse stance facing

forward **(Fig. 27)**.

Step 26: Repeat steps 24 and 25 to the right side **(Figs. 28 and 29)**. Continue to slide to the left and right ten to twenty times, each time ending in a square horse stance facing forward.

Step 27: Next, straighten up. ***Step 28***: Sink down into a left-facing rooted stance while exhaling **(Fig. 30)**. Hold this posture for thirty seconds.

Step 29: Stand up while inhaling. ***Step 30***: Sink down into a right-facing rooted stance while exhaling **(Fig. 31)**. Hold this posture for thirty seconds.

Step 31: Repeat steps 27 through 30 in rapid succession ten to twenty times.

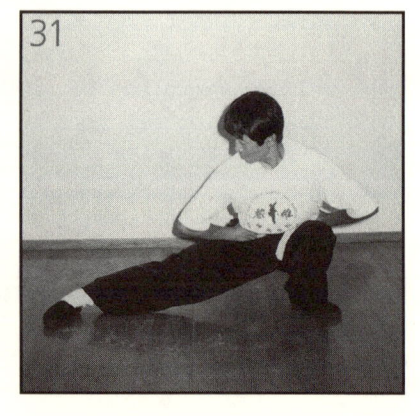

Step 32: Straighten up again. Lift your arms to shoulder level while inhaling. In a relaxed manner, shake out your arms and hands to release any tension **(Fig. 32)**. ***Step 33***: Jump up into the air, bringing your feet together and crossing your arms in front of your chest while still in midair **(Fig. 33)**. ***Step 34***: Drop to the ground, inhale deeply, and exhale deeply. ***Step 35***: Spread your feet slightly wider than shoulder width. ***Step 36***: Draw your hands up to your waist and close them into fists. ***Step 37***: Push your fists

upward so that your arms are in front of your chest. **(Fig. 34)** ***Step 38***: Keeping your legs motionless, bend forward **(Fig. 35)**. Extend your left fist to your right toe **(Fig. 36)**.

Step 39: Punch with your right fist to your left toe **(Fig. 37)**, then your left fist to your right toe, and so on. As you punch, fully rotate your shoulders and twist your waist. Keep your head in one place. Keep your back straight and do not hunch your shoulders.

Step 40: Stop punching and stretch by reaching toward the ground with your fingers. ***Step 41***: Straighten up into a standing position and bring your arms up to shoulder level while inhaling. Shake out your arms and hands.

Step 42: Repeat steps 33 and 34 in rapid succession ten to twenty times.

Step 43: Spread your feet to shoulder width. Drop your hands to your sides. ***Step 44***: Begin rotating your waist, first to the left and then to the right, in a smooth circular motion, almost as if you were spinning a hula hoop **(Figs. 38 and 39)**. Keep your head and upper body motionless. ***Step 45***: Stand on your tiptoes.

Step 46: Repeat step 44.

The Secrets of Northern Shaolin Kung-Fu

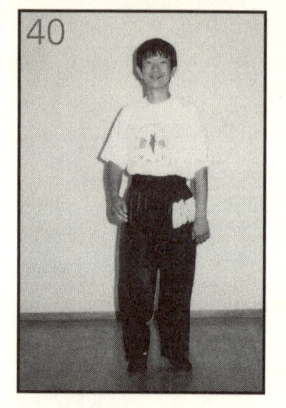

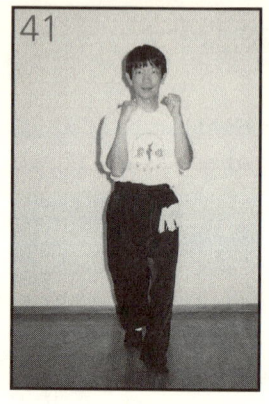

Step 47: Walk in place by alternately lifting your left heel off the ground, then lifting your right heel off the ground **(Fig. 40)**. Allow your arms to swing freely back and forth. ***Step 48***: Begin jogging in place **(Fig. 41)**. As you jog, allow your shoulders to move up and down and to rotate freely. Keep your hands locked in a fist. Keep your elbows near your body rather than allowing them to flap up and down.

Step 49: Leap into the air as you punch rapidly in front of you two to three times **(Fig. 42)**. ***Step 50***: Bring your legs inward so that your feet are together when you land. Immediately jump back into the air for a repeat of step 49. Repeat this sequence two or three more times to complete the routine.

PART FOUR
FORM AND FUNCTION

Chapter 14
Purpose of Forms Training

Many beginning students question the value of spending countless hours mastering the complicated movements that make up each form. Why, they ask, can't we just learn the bare necessities, like punching and kicking? The answer is that the inherent value of the Chinese martial arts extends far beyond the realm of physical combat. There are as many reasons for learning Chinese kung-fu as there are students of it. Naturally, some practitioners are primarily interested in self-defense, but many others study kung-fu for better health, to achieve a closer integration between mind and body, or just for the fun of it.

When it comes to health and exercise, few physical pursuits are as beneficial and all-purpose as a martial arts training program. If one simply desires to increase muscular strength and endurance, then weight lifting is an effective means of doing so. Swimming, jogging, and biking, among other activities, help to build a strong cardiovascular system. Yoga and dance greatly enhance flexibility and coordination. Martial arts practice, however, encompasses all of these areas.

Nowhere is this more apparent than in forms training. Strength, endurance, flexibility, coordination, and balance are all prerequisites for the proper execution of forms. These skills are slowly developed and honed over time through repetitive forms practice. Beginners may find that when they first begin forms training their movements are clumsy and they run out of energy before completion of a routine. Practice makes perfect, however, and even the most awkward students will eventually discover that forms training leads to noticeable improvements not only in these specific areas but also in their overall level of health.

For those who are primarily concerned with self-defense, forms training is an essential part of preparing for physical confrontation. Forms are, at their most basic level, a linked set of individual combat techniques. Each form will usually include a wide range of techniques, both offensive and defensive, including strikes, kicks, blocks, sweeps, evasive maneuvers, and grappling techniques. When executed with the proper speed and force, a form is an accurate imitation of actual fighting. The uninitiated often doubt the practicality of forms because they cannot envision the use of such seemingly elaborate techniques in combat. However, martial artists who have achieved a high level of proficiency can and do fight in this way. Unfortunately, there are few with the talent and determination to achieve such a level.

Chapter 15

Tuan Ta: Pek Sil Lum's Foundation Form

Of the ten core Pek Sil Lum forms, tuan ta (or close-distance fighting) is the most basic. Tuan ta illustrates fundamental techniques that appear again and again in the additional nine forms. These techniques include kicking, striking, simultaneous blocking and striking, sweeping, creating openings for an attack, disengaging from an opponent's grasp, attacking combinations, fighting several opponents at once, and so on. All subsequent Pek Sil Lum forms use these techniques as a foundation upon which to introduce more complicated and acrobatic maneuvers.

Within the Pek Sil Lum curriculum, tuan ta is actually the sixth form. It is usually taught first because it is one of the shortest forms and the least physically demanding. Of the ten core forms, numbers one, two, three, nine, and ten are the longest and most strenuous. When practicing these forms, one should begin with the first form and continue, without stopping, all the way through to the tenth. The easier forms are placed in the middle of the routine to give the practitioner a bit of breather between the first three forms and the final two. It is said that before Ku Ju-chang, the forms were taught in order, starting with form one. One of Ku Ju-chang's innovations was to begin the teaching with the shortest and easiest forms first.

Tuan ta is so named because it focuses on fighting opponents who are within close range. In the context of Pek Sil Lum, close range means about an arm's-length away from an opponent. As a long-distance fighting style, Pek Sil Lum emphasizes preventing attackers from moving closer than the length of one's arm—the reason being that if you can keep your opponent at that distance he won't be able to deliver any life-threatening strikes. Keeping a distance from your opponent is especially important if he is a practitioner of a grappling or close-range style such as jujutsu or Wing Chun, respectively.

When learning tuan ta, you should pay special notice to a few techniques that are an essential part of the Pek Sil Lum style. The first of these is a vertical fist strike delivered from the bow stance. The beauty of this technique lies in its simplicity. It is easy to perform, fast, and direct. You will see this strike repeatedly in the additional forms. The vertical fist strike is often made as part of the following combination of movements: step forward into a left bow stance while delivering a forward strike with your right vertical fist; at the same time, retract your right fist as you strike with a left vertical fist and deliver a forward kick with your right leg; retract your left hand and step forward into a right bow stance as you strike again with a right vertical fist. The retraction of your right leg can double as a sweep to your opponent's lead leg.

A second reccurring technique introduced in tuan ta is the forward sweep followed by the backward sweep. The forward sweep is an effective means to bring your opponent to the ground or at least to offset the stability of his footing. If your opponent is able to anticipate the forward sweep and react by retreating out of harm's way, a quick follow-up with a backward sweep will often catch him just as he lands on his feet after having moved out of range of the forward sweep. These techniques must be performed very quickly and forcefully, otherwise the opponent will be able to move in and attack while you are in an extremely vulnerable position.

A third technique to be gleaned from tuan ta is what is known in Chinese martial arts as "opening the gate." This essentially entails striking or pushing aside an opponent's guard to create an opening for your attack. There are many techniques suitable for opening the gate, but two of the simplest are featured in tuan ta. The first is the backfist/roundhouse strike technique introduced in the hand technique chapter of this book. The second technique is: As your opponent strikes with his right hand, execute a clockwise circular blocking motion with your left arm, leading with your elbow and turning your arm and body to redirect the force of his strike. If performed correctly, your opponent's right arm will be extended away from his body, providing you with an opening to strike his torso.

The best way to learn tuan ta is to practice it in sections of three to four movements at a time. Wait until you are reasonably proficient in each section before moving on to the next. Once you are comfortable with the individual sections, string them together and practice the form from beginning to end without pause. At first, your movements will be slow and somewhat awkward, but with practice you will find that you can perform the form more smoothly. Ideally, tuan ta should be performed very quickly, but without sacrificing form, balance, or power.

Description of the Form

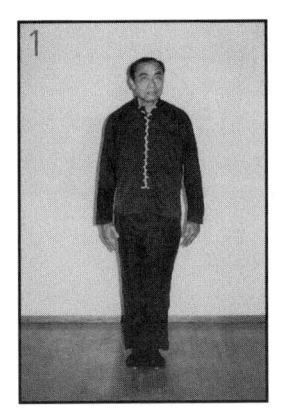

Step 1: To begin the form, start in the ready position facing north with your back straight, your eyes directed forward, your hands at your sides, and your feet together **(Fig. 1)**.

Step 2: Close your right hand into a fist and draw it up to your right ear, followed by your open left hand, as with the Pek Sil Lum bow. In this posture, both arms are held parallel to the floor. Push both hands forward to slightly below shoulder level as you bend your knees and sink down **(Figs 2 and 3)**.

Step 3: Open your right hand and touch the back of your right hand to the back of your left hand. Allow both hands to drop in a semicircular arc down to your abdomen and then draw them up to your chest, straightening your knees as you do so **(Figs. 4 and 5)**.

Step 4: Without pausing, allow your hands to continue their arcing motion out and away from your chest; downward below waist level where they separate; back toward your legs where the fingers of the right hand brush against the outside of the right thigh and the fingers of the left hand brush against the left thigh; and past your legs to the rear of your body **(Fig.**

The Secrets of Northern Shaolin Kung-Fu

6).

Step 5: Now rise to a standing position with your knees straight as you raise your arms (still behind your torso) to shoulder level **(Fig. 7)**.

Step 6: Allow your arms to continue rising until they are at full extension above your head. Now drop your arms straight down so that your hands pass along either side of your head and down the sides of your body before finally coming to rest slightly away from your hips **(Figs. 8 and 9)**. Ideally, steps 3 through 6 are performed in one smooth, coordinated motion.

Step 7: Raise your right knee so that your thigh is parallel to the floor **(Fig. 10)**. Step 8: Execute a double jumping kick with the left leg. Complete the kick with your left leg forward in a rearing horse stance. Your hands are held out to either side to help maintain your balance **(Figs. 11 and 12)**.

Step 9: Draw your hands in an inward circular motion parallel to the floor so that they come to rest against your hips with the palms directed upward **(Fig 13)**.

Step 10: Thrust your hands straight up in front of your body until your

wrists cross slightly above and in front of your forehead. Your hands should be high enough so that your forward view is not blocked by your crossed wrists **(Fig. 14)**.

Step 11: Close and form your hands into a crane beak configuration and rotate your wrists so that the fingers of each hand point forward (north) **(Fig. 15)**. ***Step 12***: Swing your hands down to either side, with the hands remaining in the crane beak posture **(Fig. 16)**.

Step 13: Retract your left foot slightly and then slide forward into a bow stance to the northwest **(Fig. 17)**. ***Step 14***: Slide forward into right bow stance to the northeast **(Fig. 18)**.

Step 15: Bring your left foot up to meet your right so that you are facing due north. As you bring your left foot forward, also bring your arms straight up in front of you in an upward strike or block that makes use of the backs of your wrists **(Fig. 19)**.

Step 16: Bend your knees and drop your arms downward so that your fingertips brush against the outside of your thighs **(Fig. 20)**.

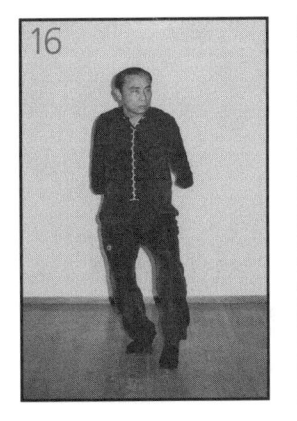

Step 17: Swing your hands out to either side and inward for a double-

fisted strike as you straighten your knees and rise to a standing posture **(Fig. 21)**.

Step 18: Draw both hands in toward your chest to gather your energy and then punch out to either side (east and west) **(Fig. 22)**. ***Step 19***: Swing both arms down toward one another until your forearms cross **(Fig. 23)**.

Step 20: Without pausing in your motion, continue to swing your right arm in the clockwise arc initiated in step 19. Your right hand will swing in front of your body in this direction more than 360 degrees until it comes to rest near your left floating rib. After meeting your right arm in the crossing motion performed in step 19, your left hand will reverse its direction to follow in a clockwise motion slightly behind the right hand until it comes to a rest in an open-handed block at your right shoulder **(Fig. 24)**. The respective movements of the right and left arms take place simultaneously so that the left hand stops at the right shoulder at the same time the right hand arrives as the left floating rib.

Step 21: Draw your right hand up near your left armpit and then shoot it across your chest to deliver a punch with a vertical fist to the east **(Fig.**

25).

Step 22: Bend both knees and sink down. Look to the west. Slide in a square horse stance to the west while punching with the left hand **(Figs. 26 and 27)**.

Step 23: Raise your left leg **(Fig. 28)**. Block downward in front of your left thigh with your left forearm **(Fig. 29)**.

Step 24: Curl your left arm across your chest in a chambering motion. Without pausing, step to the west with your left foot as you execute a hand grab to the west **(Fig. 30)**. Step around with your right foot as you sink into a square horse stance while swinging your right arm to execute a forearm block directed to the west **(Fig. 31)**. Your chest is now facing south.

Step 25: Raise your right leg as you chamber your right arm across your chest **(Figs. 32 and 33)**. Block downward in front of your right thigh with your right forearm **(Fig. 34)**.

Step 26: Place your right foot on the floor. Leading with your left elbow, step to the west with your left foot as you block in a clockwise motion with

The Secrets of Northern Shaolin Kung-Fu

your left arm **(Fig. 35)**. ***Step 27***: As you complete the clockwise blocking motion, shift into a left bow stance and punch to the west with a right vertical fist **(Fig. 36)**.

Step 28: Form a left-hand crane beak configuration and hook it over the biceps of your right arm. Bring your right foot up to meet the back of your

left foot **(Fig. 37)**. ***Step 29***: Slide your left hand rapidly down your right arm in a stripping motion as you sink down into a left-facing rooted stance **(Figs. 38 and 39)**.

Step 30: Stand up into a left bow stance, still facing west **(Fig. 40)**. ***Step 31***: Step forward with your right foot to form a right rearing horse stance while swinging your left hand upward in front of your body and drop your right hand directly down so that your hands brush against one another as they pass at the level of your abdomen. As you complete your forward step into a right rearing horse stance, your arms should be fully extended with the wrists bent **(Fig. 41)**.

Step 32: Step forward with your left foot into a left rearing horse stance, reversing the position of your arms as you do so **(Fig. 42)**.

Step 33: Lift your left leg in a chambering motion and execute a double jumping kick with your right leg **(Figs. 43 and 44)**. As your right foot extends to deliver the kick, slap the top of your foot with your right hand.

Step 34: Land with your chest facing southwest. Reach out to grab an opponent to the west **(Fig. 45)**. ***Step 35***: Pull both hands to your waist and sink into a square horse stance facing south **(Fig. 46)**.

Step 36: Execute a backfist/roundhouse strike to the west **(Fig. 47)**. ***Step 37***: Lift your right foot a few inches off the ground and stomp down on the

ground beside your left foot; as you stomp down, smash the back of your right fist into your open left hand **(Figs. 48 and 49)**.

Step 38: Draw your hands in toward your abdomen to gather your energy as you kick to the east with a modified left heel kick **(Figs. 50 and 51)**. ***Step 39***: After completing the kick, plant your left foot on the ground and sink into a square horse stance with your chest facing south and your eyes directed to the east. Slide your right foot in to meet your left foot, chamber your left leg and kick a second time to the east with a modified left heel kick. After completing the kick, plant your left foot on the ground and sink into a square horse stance with your chest facing south.

Step 40: Execute a backfist/roundhouse strike to the west **(Fig. 52)**. ***Step 41***: Turn 180 degrees into a left twisting horse stance with your chest facing north. As you turn and sink down into the twisting horse stance, smash your right fist into your left palm **(Fig. 53)**.

Step 42: Draw your hands inward to gather your energy and kick to the east a third time with a modified right heel kick **(Fig. 54)**. After completing the kick, plant your right foot on the ground and sink into a square horse

stance with your chest facing north.

Step 43: Execute a backfist/roundhouse strike to the east **(Fig. 55)**.
Step 44: Execute a cleaving block/strike to the west **(Fig. 56)**. ***Step 45***: Execute a cleaving block/strike to the east **(Fig. 57)**.

Step 46: Turn your hips to the left (north). As you turn, allow your extended left arm to come to the center of your body with the fist held upright. Bring your right arm in to meet your left forearm. Sink down into a square horse stance facing north as you simultaneously lift your right forearm up to form a block in front of your forehead and drop your left arm down to a position above your left knee **(Fig. 58)**. Your arms should cross directly in front of your torso before they are extended into their respective blocking postures.

Step 47: Pivot on your right foot as you turn to face west in a left rearing horse stance. As you

turn, bring your right arm down to brush along your left arm in a blocking motion. Without pausing the downward motion of your arms, allow them to swing out to either side of your body **(Fig. 59)**.

Step 48: Bring your arms inward to brush against one another **(Fig. 60)**.

Step 49: Step back with your left foot as your right arm circles in a clockwise motion in front of your body **(Fig. 61)**. As in step 20, the left arm follows behind the right arm in a clockwise circular motion.

Step 50: Step back with your right foot and sink down into a left rearing horse as your arms complete their clockwise motion and come to rest with your forearms crossed in front of your torso in a blocking posture **(Fig. 62)**.

Step 51: Drop your hands and brush the fingertips of your left hand across the outside of your left thigh and the fingertips of your right hand across the inside of your left thigh. Then swing both hands upward rapidly so that your right hand forms an open-handed block in front of your forehead while your left arm extends to the south with the left hand in a crane beak configuration **(Fig. 63)**.

Step 52: Turn your shoulders and head toward the east. Extend both

arms and reach out to grab with your hands **(Fig. 64)**. ***Step 53***: Draw your hands in toward your abdomen as you whip your right leg around to the west in a forward sweep. Come to a stop in a right rooted stance with your right leg extended to the west **(Figs. 65 and 66)**.

Step 54: Place both hands on the ground and swing your left leg around 180 degrees to the west in a backward sweep **(Fig. 67)**. ***Step 55***: Allow your left leg to continue its motion so that it extends to the south.

Step 56: Hop up into a square horse stance facing west. Swing your left arm in front of your body in a clockwise blocking motion, leading with your elbow, as you hop **(Fig. 68)**. As your left arm rotates up to block above your head, punch to the west with a right vertical fist **(Fig. 69)**.

Step 57: Shift into a bow stance facing north as you push your left hand down to protect your groin and draw your right hand to your waist **(Fig. 70)**.

Step 58: Shift your hips to the west and rise to a standing posture. As you rise, punch to the west with a right vertical fist **(Fig. 71)**. Your left hand retracts to form an open-handed block at your right shoulder **(Fig. 72)**.

Step 59: Slip your left hand to the outside of your right arm **(Fig. 73)**.

The Secrets of Northern Shaolin Kung-Fu

Step 60: Sink into a twisting horse stance with your upper torso facing north as you cross your arms in front of your chest. ***Step 61***: At the same time, kick and punch to the west as you punch to the east **(Fig. 74)**.

Step 62: Step forward into a left bow stance facing west as you retract your hands and then punch to the southeast with your left hand and to the west with your right hand **(Figs. 75 and 76)**.

Step 63: Execute a figure-eight motion with your right arm in the following manner: drop your right hand down to the right side of your body, along the outside of your thigh; allow it to continue swinging upward until it is slightly higher than your right shoulder; swing it in a diagonal downward arc from the upper right side of your body to the lower left side of your body, to the outside of your left thigh; from the left side of your body swing your arm up to your left shoulder; finally, swing your arm in a diagonal downward arc across your body to the front of your groin **(Fig. 77)**.

Step 64: Kick to the west with a right toe kick **(Fig. 78)**. ***Step 65***: As your right leg completes the kick, plant your right foot forward and sink down into a right rooted stance with your right arm extended toward your foot

and your left arm extended behind you **(Figs. 79 and 80)**. Notice that your arms are in alignment.

Step 66: Bring your left foot up to meet your right foot as you rise to a standing posture and rotate your entire body 180 degrees so that you are facing east. Your left arm will be extended upward above your head, while your right arm will be held down alongside your right thigh **(Fig. 81)**.

Step 67: Drop your left arm in a semicircular motion across the centerline of your body and then to the left of your torso. As your arm crosses to the left of your torso, swing your right arm across your body in a blocking motion **(Figs. 82 and 83)**.

Step 68: Drop your right arm to the right side of your torso and swing your left arm across in a blocking motion **(Fig. 84)**. ***Step 69***: Bring both hands to the front of your body with your left hand above and your right hand below, as if you were carrying a large ball **(Fig. 85)**.

Step 70: Simultaneously push your left hand downward and pull your right hand up to the posi-

tion shown **(Fig. 86)**. As your right arm reaches full extension, turn your right palm to face outward.

Step 71: Kick to the east with a left toe kick **(Fig. 87)**. ***Step 72***: As you complete the kick, plant your left foot forward and shift into a left bow stance.

Step 73: Brush your arms against one another in a downward blocking motion **(Fig. 88)**.

Step 74: Chamber both hands at the left side of your waist. Lift your right foot slightly, then stamp the ground with your right foot while at the same time extend your left leg forward. As you extend your left leg, execute a backfist strike to the east with your right hand.

Step 75: Chamber both hands at the right side of your waist **(Fig. 89)**. ***Step 76***: Execute a backfist strike to the east with your left hand followed by a punch with a right vertical fist as you step forward into a left bow stance **(Fig. 90)**. ***Step 77***: Punch to the east with a left vertical fist as you kick in the same direction with your right leg **(Fig. 91)**.

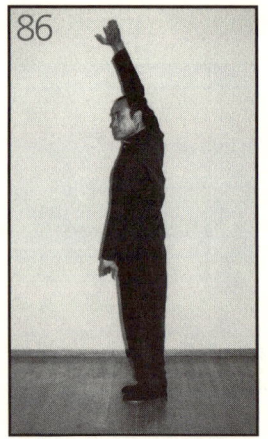

Step 78: Drop your right foot forward into a right bow stance as you

punch to the east with a right vertical fist **(Fig. 92)**.

Step 79: Curl your right arm inward toward your chest in a chambering motion. Step to the southeast with the left foot as you bring your hands up in a blocking/striking posture **(Figs. 93 and 94)**.

Step 80: Pivot on your left foot as you turn your torso to the north and simultaneously stomp with your right foot and punch downward to the east with your right fist **(Figs. 95 and 96)**. Your right arm will now be extended to the east and your chest will be facing to the north.

Step 81: Execute a tornado kick to the south **(Fig. 97)**. ***Step 82***: Land in a square horse stance facing north. Execute a clockwise circular block with your left arm as you simultaneously punch with a right vertical fist to the north **(Figs. 98 and 99)**.

The Secrets of Northern Shaolin Kung-Fu

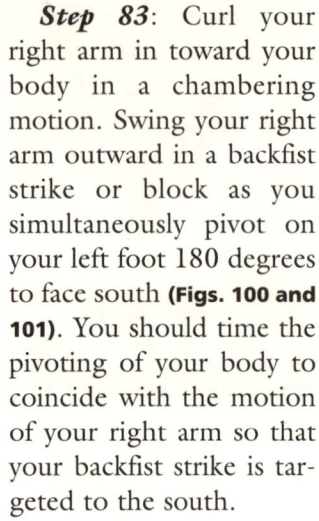

Step 83: Curl your right arm in toward your body in a chambering motion. Swing your right arm outward in a backfist strike or block as you simultaneously pivot on your left foot 180 degrees to face south **(Figs. 100 and 101)**. You should time the pivoting of your body to coincide with the motion of your right arm so that your backfist strike is targeted to the south.

Step 84: Slice down and forward with a knife hand strike as you retract your right hand to behind your right ear **(Figs. 102 and 103)**. ***Step 85***: Execute an overhand backfist strike with your right hand as you retract your left hand to an open-handed blocking position near your right shoulder **(Figs. 104 and 105)**. ***Step 86***: Execute a second knife hand strike with your left hand as you draw your right hand to your waist **(Figs. 106 and 107)**. *Step 87*: Punch with a right horizontal fist to the south as you retract your left hand to an open-handed blocking position near your right shoulder **(Figs. 108 and 109)**.

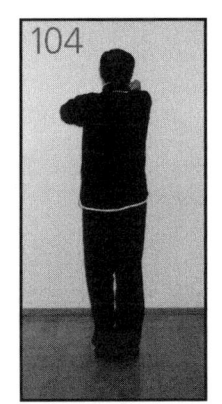

Step 88: Chamber your hands at the right side of your waist. Lift your right foot slightly. Simultaneously stamp the ground with your right foot while extending your left leg to the east as you execute a backfist strike to the east with your left hand. Step forward to the east into a left bow stance as you punch with a right vertical fist **(Fig. 110)**.

Step 89: Deliver a simultaneous punch and kick to the east **(Fig. 111)**. *Step 90*: After completing the kick, plant your right foot forward and shift into a right bow stance as you punch to the east with a right vertical fist **(Fig. 112)**.

Step 91: Swing your right arm across your body at chest level. As your arm reaches the center of your body (facing north), shift into a square horse stance. As your arm continues around to the left of your body (facing west), shift into a left bow stance and punch to the west with a left vertical fist **(Fig. 113)**.

***Step** 92*: Take a small step to the west with your left foot as you punch with a right vertical fist to the west **(Fig. 114)**.

***Step** 93*: Repeat step 92.

***Step** 94*: Take a small step the west with your left foot and punch with your right hand to the west while extending your left hand to the southeast **(Fig. 115)**.

***Step** 95*: Swing your left fist up and over to meet your right fist **(Fig. 116)**. ***Step** 96*: Swing to the left to wind up for a backfist/roundhouse strike **(Fig. 117)**.

Step 97: Execute a backfist/roundhouse strike to the east **(Fig. 118)**. ***Step** 98*: Follow with a cleaving block/strike to the west **(Fig. 119)**. ***Step** 99*: Execute a cleaving block/strike to the east **(Fig. 120)**.

***Step** 100*: Repeat step 46.

Step** 101*: Step back (south) with your left foot as you draw your hands inward **(Fig. 121)**. ***Step** 102*: Step back with your right foot so that it meets your left foot (but your knees remain bent) as you draw both hands toward your abdomen with the backs of your hands touching. ***Step 103: Rise into a standing position with your knees straight as you draw your hands upward toward your chest **(Fig. 122)**.

Step 104: Without pausing, allow your hands to continue their arcing motion out and away from your chest; downward below waist level where they separate; back toward your legs where the fingers of the right hand brush against the outside of the right thigh and the fingers of the left hand brush against the left thigh; and past your legs to the rear of your body **(Fig. 123)**.

Step 105: Now rise to a standing position with your knees straight as you raise your arms (still behind your torso) to shoulder level with the fingers of each hand pointed downward and the palms facing out to either side.

Step 106: Draw your hands up and behind you until your arms are at full

extension above your head; then drop them straight down to pass along either side of your head, continuing down the sides of your body, coming to a rest slightly away from your hips **(Fig. 124)**.

Step 107: Close your right hand into a fist and draw it up to your right ear, followed by your open left hand, as with the Pik Sil Lum bow. In this posture, both arms are held parallel to the floor. Push both hands forward to slightly below shoulder level as you bend your knees and sink down **(Fig. 125)**.

Step 108: Rise to standing position and drop your hands loosely to your sides **(Fig. 126)**.

Step 109: Bow **(Fig. 127)**.

Chapter 16
Applications of Tuan Ta

Scholars of Chinese martial arts often analyze the art of fighting according to the various skills or tactics one might employ in a combat situation. The specific skills used may vary depending upon the particular style, but in general they include kicking (attacking the enemy with the legs or feet), striking (attacking with the hands, fingers, palms, or other portion of the upper limbs), throwing (wrestling or bringing the enemy to the ground), catching (capturing the enemy in a joint lock or hold), pouncing (offensive or defensive tumbling techniques), pushing (using explosive force), and bumping (close-range attacks using the knee, elbow, waist, shoulder, or head). Fighting tactics include opening the gate (creating an opening in the enemy's guard for your attack), charging (a forward rushing attack), pressing (engaging in close-range fighting), shifting (moving to the side or rear of the enemy), advancing and retreating, dodging, and leaping (attacking the enemy while in midair). Without exception, all these skills and tactics are contained within tuan ta.

Most of the techniques introduced in tuan ta have more than one self-defense application. Some applications are immediately obvious, while others usually require an explanation from an instructor. In more traditional times, it was not uncommon for an instructor to leave it up to the individual student to figure out the practical applications concealed within the forms. Practice the form one thousand times, an instructor might say, and then you will begin to understand its practical application.

Times change, however, and in recognition of this fact we provide an explanation of the primary applications of tuan ta below.

As you learn this form, remain mindful of the applications for each sequence of movements. Concentrate on performing each movement with the force or speed necessary for its successful application in a fighting situation. Otherwise, your exertions will amount to little more than a pretty, but useless, form of dancing.

Tuan Ta Techniques

In the following photographs, applications of tuan ta are illustrated by the person in the white shirt.

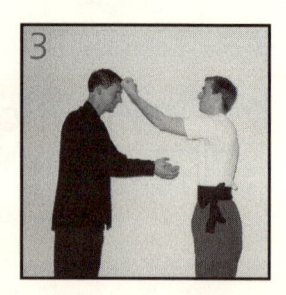

The Secrets of Northern Shaolin Kung-Fu

Steps 1 and 2: Begin in a neutral ready position, ready to respond to an attack from any direction. The elaborate Pek Sil Lum bow is more symbolic than practical—it demonstrates respect for your opponent before the commencement of hostilities and identifies you as a student of the Pek Sil Lum school. If your opponent were to attack as you bowed, however, you would still be in a posture suited to a quick response.

Step 3: Turn both hands palms outward. In a downward arc, draw them toward your lower abdomen and then sharply upward; this allows you to break free of a wrist hold **(Figs. 1 and 2)**.

Step 4: Continue building upon the momentum of your circular arm motion to deliver a double-fisted strike with the back of your hands to your opponent's head **(Fig. 3)**. Steps 3 and 4 should be executed in one fluid motion so that you jerk your hands away from a hold, pulling your opponent forward and slightly off-balance in the process, and then immediately follow up with a backfist strike. Next, drop your hands down to brush past your thighs, warding off kicks or strikes from either side.

Note: The following expansive arm motion allows you to simultaneously fill your lungs with air and to defend the space around your torso and head from attacks on either side.

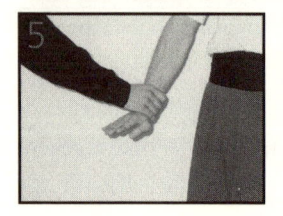

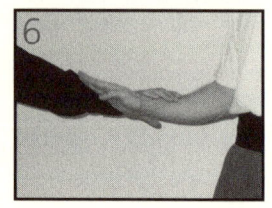

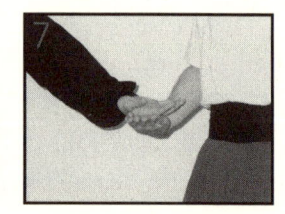

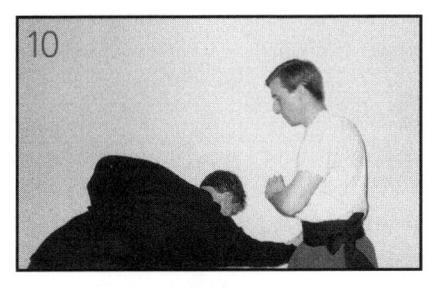

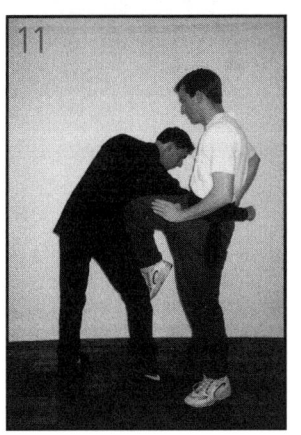

Steps 5 and 6: Strike an opponent to the north with a double jumping kick **(Fig. 4)**.

Step 7: Rotate your hands in a circular motion inward to your waist to execute a simple escape from a wrist hold applied from either side **(Figs. 5–7)**.

Step 8: Thrust both hands upward to block an overhead blow to the head **(Fig. 8)**.

Steps 9 and 10: Hook inward with your hands, catching hold of the attacker's wrist with your opposite hand (e.g., if he strikes with his right hand, grasp his right wrist with your right hand); pull him forward and to the side so that he falls to the ground **(Figs. 9 and 10)**. Alternatively, instead of pulling him to the ground, you can jerk him toward you as you strike to his groin or stomach with your knee **(Fig. 11)**. If you are pulling him with your right hand, strike him with your right knee and vice versa.

Step 11: Propel yourself forward toward your opponent to the north. If he is facing you with his left leg forward, hook your left leg behind his left leg and sweep backward with your leg as you push him backward **(Figs. 12 and 13)**. If executed correctly, your opponent will flip backward and hit the ground with his head or back.

Note: This following maneuver has the same application as step 11, but uses the opposite leg.

Step 12: Bring your arms directly forward and up as you rise to a standing position—the combined momentum of your arms and body moving in concert allows you to generate a great deal of force for a top-wrist strike (or block) **(Fig. 14)**. If you choose to strike with the back of your wrist, aim for the underside of your opponent's jaw.

Step 13: Sink downward as you brush your hands against your thighs in a blocking maneuver. This movement has several purposes: In addition to warding off potential attacks from either side, it allows you to "open a gate" for the next technique by moving your opponent's arms down toward his waist, and it enables you to generate force for the following strike **(Figs. 15 and 16)**.

Step 14: Without stopping the arm motion initiated in step 13, bring both hands up and inward for a double-fisted strike to your opponent's head **(Fig. 17)**. As you bring your arms up for the strike, rise to a standing position to fully bring the force of your entire body behind the double-fisted attack.

Step 15: Pull hands inward toward the chest and punch attackers simultaneously to the West and the East. Notice that the combination of steps 14 and 15 depicts a situation in which you are defending yourself from at least three separate attackers (to the north, east, and west).

Step 16: Swing your forearms down toward one another until they cross to smash away a wrist hold applied by an opponent or to intercept a low strike **(Fig. 18)**.

Steps 17 and 18: Continue the arm motion initiated in step 16 to deliver an unexpected strike to the East. The clockwise circular motion of your arms can be used as a blocking motion and serves to generate force for a powerful eastward punch.

Step 19: Sink down and propel yourself to the west in a square horse stance to strike an opponent in that direction **(Figs. 19 and 20)**.

Step 20: Raise your left leg to protect your groin. Swing your left arm downward to block a kick **(Fig. 21)**.

Step 21: Chamber your arm and deliver a backfist strike to the west. Without pausing, step to the west and pivot 180 degrees as you bring your right forearm around to execute a block **(Fig. 22)**. Alternatively, use the back-

The Secrets of Northern Shaolin Kung-Fu

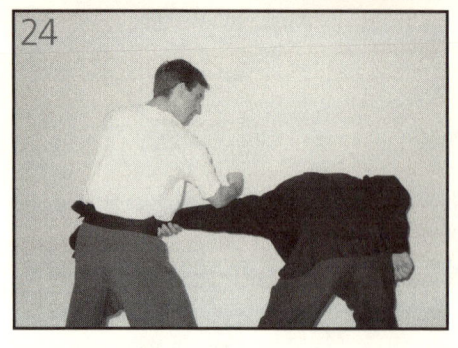

fist to strike away your opponent's guard that you can step around and strike him w a right hammer fist to the side of the he If your opponent has his left arm forwa the backfist motion can also serve as a g to your opponent's left wrist in preparat for a joint lock. Once you have reached to grasp your opponent's left wrist w your left hand, step down with your left f and pivot 180 degrees as you bring y right arm across to rest against your op nent's left elbow **(Figs. 23 and 24)**. Wit tight hold on his wrist, exert downw pressure on the elbow to execute a jo lock. If you execute this sequence quic and strike the elbow forcefully with y forearm, you can break it.

Step 22: Raise your leg to protect y groin, chamber your right arm and swin downward to block a kick.

Steps 23 and 24: Place your right f on the floor. Leading with your elbow, step to the west with your left foot as y block with your left arm in a clockwise direction in front of your body **(Fig. 25)**. T motion redirects an incoming strike delivered by your opponent and creates opening for the following counterstrike with your right fist **(Fig. 26)**.

Steps 25 and 26: If your opponent grasps your right wrist, step forward with y right leg and then sink rapidly down and backward into a rooted stance as you sim taneously slide your hooked left hand along your right arm **(Figs. 27–29)**. The co bined stripping motion of your left hand and sinking down into a rooted stance enable you to remove a wrist h applied by a much stronger op nent. Also, you can sink into a ro ed stance to avoid a kick **(Fig. 30**

Steps 27 and 28: Stand up int bow stance facing west. The n sequence of movements is p formed in rapid succession—s forward into a right rearing ho stance while swinging your a past one another to protect aga kicks or punches—without pausi step into a left rearing horse stance and reverse arm positions; alternatively, rather than simply stepping forward into a right and left rearing horse stance, you can deliver two rapid kicks to your opponent's groin **(Figs. 31 and 32)**. Immediately follow up by chambering your left leg and executing a double jumping kick with your right leg **(Fig. 33)**. Ideally, you should perform this entire sequence without any break between movements. This allows you to both ward off any attacks and build momentum for a powerful double jumping kick. In addition, the rapid forward movement and expansive arm motion will confuse your opponent so that he won't be able to anticipate the double jumping kick.

Steps 30 and 31: Now that your opponent to the west is reeling from your rapid and disorienting offensive, seize him by the arm or the front of his shirt and throw him to the ground.

The Secrets of Northern Shaolin Kung-Fu

Step 32: Use a backfist to strike another opponent to the west or finish off the original opponent if your attempt at throwing him to the ground failed **(Fig. 34)**. Aim for your opponent's jaw, temple, or, especially, the fragile ridge of the cheekbone.

Step 33: Reach out and grasp the wrist of an attacker to the south. Twist it counterclockwise to create tension and then smash your right fist downward on his wrist or elbow **(Fig. 35)**. At the same time, deliver a low stomp to his foot, ankle, or shin.

Steps 34 and 35: Gather your energy inward by drawing your hands in toward your abdomen. Kick an attacker to the east twice in rapid succession **(Fig. 36)**.

Step 36: Turn back to deliver a backfist strike to the west.

Step 37: Turn 180 degrees to the north, repeating the wrist-breaking technique executed in step 33.

Step 38: Lash out with a surprise kick to the east.

Steps 39 to 41: From a square horse stance, shift to deliver a backfist strike to the east. Now deliver a backfist to the west, followed by a block or strike with your forearm or the bottom of your fist (p'i ch'uan). Notice that as you execute the cleaving block/strike to the west, your left arm swings behind to guard your rear **(Fig.**

37). In an actual combat situation, you may convert your backfist to a wrist grab and maintain a hold on your opponent's wrist as you swing your right arm across to execute a joint lock or break as in step 21. Deliver a second cleaving block/strike to the east.

Step 42: Cross your arms in a blocking motion and come to rest in a solid defensive position. You can pause here to gather your breath.

Step 43: Turn to the west, brushing your forearms forcefully against one another as you do so to strike away wrist or arm holds.

Steps 44 to 47: This complicated set of arm movements serves to ward off potential wrist holds or strikes executed by an opponent to the west. After your hands meet in front of your chest in a blocking posture, drop them down to brush alongside your left thigh, again warding off potential attack from either side.

Step 48: Turn to the east to block a strike or grasp an opponent's arm **(Fig. 38)**.

Step 49: This sequence can be used to either pull an opponent to the ground or to sweep the legs out from under an opponent to the west **(Fig. 39)**.

Step 50: Execute a backward sweep with your left leg to the west. Steps 49 and 50 can be executed in rapid succession to sweep an opponent who retreats in response to your initial attempt at a forward sweep.

Steps 51 and 52: After reorienting yourself to the west, hop up into a horse stance and swing your left arm, as in steps 23 and 24, to create an opening for a strike with your right hand.

Steps 53 and 54: Block a groin kick and counterattack with a punch **(Figs. 40 and 41)**.

Steps 55 to 57: If an opponent applies a wrist hold, turn to the north as you sink into a twisting horse stance **(Figs. 42 and 43)**. As you turn and sink, place your left forearm in front of your right forearm. Rise up as you rapidly brush your left forearm along your right forearm from elbow to wrist to strip away a wrist or arm hold. As you complete the simultaneous rising and stripping motion, kick and punch to the east and west. You can also swing your left hand forward as you rise to push away or grasp an opponent's forward arm, thus opening a gate for your kicking attack **(Fig. 44)**.

Step 58: Step into a bow stance to the west as you strike enemies to the west and southeast **(Fig. 45)**.

Step 59: Swing your right arm in a figure-eight motion to block attacks to your torso. As your fist swings down to protect your groin, you can apply a backfist strike to the shin of an opponent who is attempting to kick this vulnerable area **(Fig. 46)**.

Steps 60 and 61: Deliver a kick to the west while still protecting your groin **(Fig. 47)**. Immediately sink into a rooted stance with both arms extended to avoid a roundhouse or crescent kick from an opponent to the west.

Step 62: Bring your left foot up to meet your right foot as you rise to a standing position and rotate your body 180 degrees to face east.

Steps 63 and 64: Drop your left arm down in a semicircular motion across the centerline of your body and then to the left side of your torso to block a forward strike from an opponent to the east. Swing your right arm across your body in a blocking motion to block another forward strike from your opponent **(Fig. 48)**. Block in the same manner a third time with your left arm **(Fig. 49)**.

Step 65: Bring both hands to the front of your body as if you are holding a large ball. From this defensive stance you can execute a variety of blocking maneuvers. This posture is also used to gather one's ch'i at the center of the body.

Steps 66 to 68: Drop your left hand down to protect your groin and draw your right hand up to protect your head. Kick to the east and step forward into a bow stance.

Step 69: Brush your forearms together with sufficient force to strip off arm or wrist holds **(Fig. 50)**.

Steps 70 to 72: Chamber both hands on the left side of your waist. Lift your right foot slightly, then stamp the ground with your right foot while extending your left leg forward in a rearing horse stance. As you do so, attack your opponent to the east with a backfist strike from your right hand, or use the backfist to hit away his guard in preparation for the following technique **(Fig. 51)**. Now chamber your hands on the right of your waist and deliver a second backfist strike to the east with your left hand. If you were successful in opening a gate for attack, use this follow-up strike to hit your opponent across the nose, jaw, or cheek **(Fig. 52)**. Now step forward into a left bow stance as you execute a vertical fist punch with your right hand **(Fig. 53)**.

Step 73: Simultaneously punch and kick an opponent to the east. Even if your opponent manages to block one of your attacks, the other may hit its mark **(Fig. 54)**.

Step 74: Step forward and deliver another punch to the east **(Fig. 55)**. Alternatively, if your opponent moved in on you when you executed the kick in step 73 so that his right leg is now positioned to the rear of your right leg, you can sweep him by placing your right foot behind his right foot and swinging your leg backward (to the west) as you push him off-balance (to the east or northeast) **(Figs. 56–58)**.

Step 75: This sequence can be used to block or strike to the southeast. The open left hand can be closed into a fist for an uppercut to your opponent's midsection or the fingers can be driven into your opponent's groin from underneath **(Fig. 59)**. Or, you can clutch your opponent's genitals and

exert pressure. Notice that your right arm swings up to protect your head as you move in for this low attack.

Step 76: Pivot on your left foot as you turn your torso to the north and attack an opponent to the east by simultaneously stomping his foot, ankle, or shin with your right foot while punching downward to his leg or midsection **(Figs. 60–62)**. As you strike downward, sink into a low stance to increase the force of your blow.

Step 77: Execute a tornado kick to strike an opponent to the south. This is not the most practical technique for a real combat situation. Yet it can take an opponent to the rear completely by surprise.

Step 78: Land in a square horse stance facing north and execute a clockwise block with your left arm to open a gate for a punch with your right arm.

Step 79: Chamber your right arm to generate momentum and whip it out in a backfist strike or block to the rear as you pivot 180 degrees to face south **(Fig. 63)**.

Steps 80 to 83: Retract your right hand as you execute a downward knife hand **(Fig. 64)**. The knife hand can serve to block or trap your opponent's arm, or as a strike. Follow with an overhead strike to the bridge of your opponent's nose **(Fig. 65)**. Deliver a second knife hand to the throat **(Fig. 66)**, and then a forward punch **(Fig. 67)**. This rapid series of combinations is difficult to defend against, especially when executed with great speed at close range.

Step 84: Chamber both hands at the right side of your waist. Lift your right foot slightly, then simultaneously stamp the ground with your right foot while extending your left leg to the east. As you do so, attack the opponent to the east with a backfist strike using your left hand, then immediately follow up by stepping forward into a bow stance and executing a forward punch **(Figs. 68 and 69)**. The backfist strike can either serve as an attack or as a means to smash an opponent's arm to the side, thereby creating an opening for the forward punch.

Step 85: Continue your assault with a simultaneous left punch/right kick **(Fig. 70)**.

Step 86: Step forward with your kicking leg as you deliver a right punch.

Combine the stepping motion with the punch to generate momentum and force behind your attack. As with step 74, this sequence can also be converted into a sweep.

Step 87: Without bending your elbow, swing your arm in a straight line across your body at chest level. As the arm travels to the center of your body, shift into a square horse stance. As your arm reaches the left side of your body, shift into a left bow stance and punch the opponent to the west with your left hand **(Fig. 71)**.

Steps 88 and 89: Take a small step to the west with your left foot and punch the same opponent with your right hand **(Fig. 72)**. Take another small step with your left foot and punch him again with your left hand. Note that after having punched your opponent with your right arm, you can keep the arm extended to create a "bridge" to your opponent's arm as a means of controlling his guard in preparation for the following strike with your left hand.

Steps 90 and 91: Repeat steps 88 and 89.

Step 92: This is a slight variation on step 88. This time you attack in two

directions simultaneously—to the west with your right hand and to the southeast with your left hand.

Step 93: Bring your left fist up and over to rest on top of your right fist. This can serve as a strike to the hand of an opponent who has grasped your right wrist, or as a simple strike to his cheek or jaw **(Figs. 73 and 74)**.

Steps 94 and 95: Twist to the left and immediately execute a backfist strike to the opponent sneaking up from the east **(Figs. 75 and 76)**.

Steps 96 and 97: Defend against attackers to the west and east with a series of rapidly executed cleaving block/strike.

Step 98: As you sink into a square horse stance facing north, cross your arms in front of your body in standard blocking motion. Your right hand continues upward to protect your head and your left hand comes to rest above your left knee. This is a strong, easily defensible position in which you can rest and gather your energy.

Steps 99 and 100: Step back (south) with your left foot as you draw your hands inward. Step back with your right foot so that it meets your left foot as you draw your hands toward your abdomen. This motion enables you to

The Secrets of Northern Shaolin Kung-Fu

fill your lungs with oxygen and to gather your energy.

Step 101: Stand up straight as your hands continue their upward arc to your chest.

Step 102: Sink down as your hands arc downward to brush along the outside of your thighs, warding off kicks or strikes from either side.

Steps 103 and 104: The following expansive arm motion allows you to both fill your lungs with air and to defend the space around your torso and head from attacks on either side.

Steps 105 and 106: Perform the Pek Sil Lum bow. Rise to a standing position and drop your hands loosely to your sides.

Step 107: Bow to close the form.

Afterword

We would like to emphasize that no book is an adequate teacher. Not only will many of the important subtleties of Pek Sil Lum be passed over if one depends solely on a book for instruction, but in some cases readers will learn to perform a technique incorrectly and perhaps harm his or her body in the process. We encourage you to treat this work as an introduction to the basic physical and theoretical aspects of Pek Sil Lum kung-fu rather than a complete guide. We highly recommend that you seek a qualified instructor if you are serious about mastering this or any other style of martial art.

That said, if you master the techniques presented in this book (under the supervision of an instructor) you will be well on your way to becoming an accomplished practitioner of Pek Sil Lum. The various skills we have presented here are all authentic, essential components of Pek Sil Lum as it has been taught since Ku Ju-chang's time and perhaps long before that. As stated in the introduction, each individual instructor may vary the curriculum somewhat, but the core skills taught in a Pek Sil Lum school are fully presented herein.

There is only one way to master any martial system—kung-fu. Here, kung-fu is used in its true sense, that of "perfection achieved through exertion." It is impossible to become a martial arts expert by sitting on your couch with a book in your hand. You have to get up and do it—and do it over and over until you get it right. For beginners, we suggest a practice schedule, under a qualified instructor's supervision, of two or three times a week. You may be tempted to learn as many of the forms and fancy maneuvers as soon as possible, but the secret to any style is always in the basics—stances, footwork, and fundamental techniques such as blocking, kicking, striking, and so on. These are the pillars upon which you will base your more advanced skills. Without mastering these, your kung-fu will never reach its full potential.

Regardless of your reasons for studying the Chinese martial arts, if you follow a path of dedicated practice, the benefits you accrue will be numerous. On the physical side, these include increased flexibility and endurance; improved strength, coordination, and speed; an enhanced awareness of your body; and an overall improvement in general health.

The positive effects of practicing the martial arts, however, extend far beyond the physical realm. There is a saying common to many cultures: "healthy mind, healthy body." Although there has been a tendency in the West, since the time of the Renaissance, to emphasize the separateness of the body and what we may informally call "the mind," even Western scientists are now realizing just how important the relationship is between our physical selves and our emotional or mental condition. The Chinese have, since the time of Lao Tzu, six centuries before the common era, viewed all components of the universe as interdependent parts of the greater whole. In this conceptualization, the universe is like an infinite pool of water. Even a tiny pebble dropped into the very center of this vast pool will cause a ripple that will eventually pass through every drop of water in the pool. This analogy holds true for humans, who were often envisioned in the musings of Taoists as microcosms that mirrored the structure of the infinite universe. In this context, the mind and body were seen as interrelated components of human existence—thus, whatever phenomena affected the mind would also affect the body, and vice versa.

Much of the philosophy upon which the more esoteric aspects of the Chinese martial arts are based focuses on the concept that a proper integration of the mind and body will benefit one's health and increase longevity. There are many examples of how the mind/body relationship can be harnessed to bring about better health. For instance, most physicians now believe that regular physical exercise helps alleviate the symptoms of emotional stress, which is a major contributor to high blood pressure, heart problems, and other life-threatening conditions. Many Chinese styles also engage in static or moving meditation with the aim of clearing the mind of unwanted, unhealthy, or harmful thoughts and mental debris that might have a detrimental effect on one's health and general well-being. Even modern psychologists and psychiatrists use meditation techniques to treat patients who have low self-esteem or who have a habit of thinking in a self-defeating manner.

The Chinese martial arts help one to achieve a closer integration of the mind and body in a variety of ways. The first of these is to train an individual to become better aware of his or her physical self. Through the repetitive practice of stances, footwork, forms, and techniques, you will come to notice certain facts about your physical state that you were not mindful of previously. For example, do you walk with your feet splayed or pigeon-toed? Do you maintain upright posture or do you have a tendency to hunch your shoulders? When you breath, do you fill your lungs fully with air, or do you have a habit of breathing shallowly? Once you have increased your own awareness of your body, you can take steps to make adjustments to your posture, breathing and so on as needed. Perhaps most important, the Chinese martial arts provide training in how to regulate the flow of ch'i throughout the body. This is achieved by holding certain postures, controlling one's breathing, and concentrating on directing the flow of ch'i through meridians or to specific body parts. Even if one does not fully believe in the concept of ch'i as a vital force that regulates the processes of life, creating a mental picture of ch'i moving about in your body and learning to control the flow of this "mental ch'i" will serve to harmonize the relationship between your mind and body.

When you first begin to practice the martial arts, you will most likely have a difficult time properly executing techniques and movements. Even though your instructor explains the proper form to you, and you understand intellectually what is required, you just won't be able to get your body to follow your commands. With a great deal of practice, however, your body will begin to respond automatically according to your wishes. The automatic interaction between will, or the mind's intent, and the correct response on the part of the body is an important step on the path to mastery of the martial arts. When perfected, this connectedness reaches a state in which all thought and action are completely instantaneous and appropriate for the situation. A person who has achieved such a state could well be considered a "master."

There is a story told by the great Taoist philosopher Chuang Tze that illustrates perfectly the essence of kung-fu. The story concerns a cook named Ting who was butchering an ox for a local aristocrat named Lord Wen-hui. Lord Wen-hui noticed that Cook Ting cut through the ox with exceptional ease and complimented him on his skill. Cook Ting explained that when he first became a cook, he hacked and chopped at oxen like everybody else. With time and practice, however, he learned to guide his blade through the empty spaces between the bones, ligaments, muscles, and joints using only spirit and an understanding of the natural way of things. As a result, even after nineteen years of daily use, his knife had never become dulled or chipped. Replied Lord Wen-hui, "Now I understand the secret to caring for life!"[9]

Cook Ting is the epitome of a kung-fu master. Through time, effort, and concentration he has perfected a skill—that of butchering oxen. Once this level of skill has been achieved, however, the skill itself is transcended and becomes of secondary importance: what really matters is an understanding of the way of things.

Such are the martial arts—a physical pursuit that transcends the merely physical and points to "the Way." In the context of Chuang Tze's parable, the martial arts are a butcher's knife: When you first take up the knife, you find it awkward and difficult to use, so you hack. With practice and effort, you slowly learn to cut. After many years of kung-fu, however—zip! zoop! zing!—all is in perfect rhythm. And then you can wipe the knife and put it away, for you have finally learned how to care for life.

For more information about the Lai Hung Chinese Martial Arts Institute, please visit our homepage on the internet: http://www.dcn.davis.ca.us/~mgmarkp/lhcmai.html

Group photo: Gary Tang (left), Lai Hung (seated), Mark Poppendiek (center), Brian Klingborg (right)

Lineage

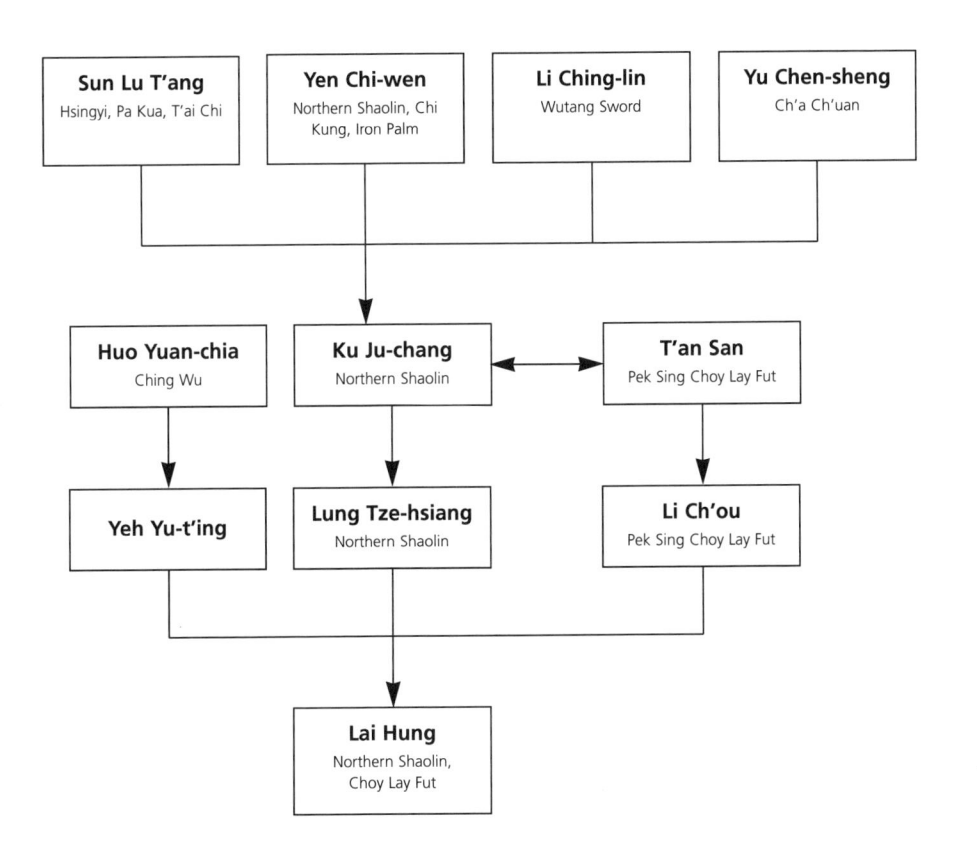

- **Sun Lu T'ang** — Hsingyi, Pa Kua, T'ai Chi
- **Yen Chi-wen** — Northern Shaolin, Chi Kung, Iron Palm
- **Li Ching-lin** — Wutang Sword
- **Yu Chen-sheng** — Ch'a Ch'uan

- **Huo Yuan-chia** — Ching Wu
- **Ku Ju-chang** — Northern Shaolin
- **T'an San** — Pek Sing Choy Lay Fut

- **Yeh Yu-t'ing**
- **Lung Tze-hsiang** — Northern Shaolin
- **Li Ch'ou** — Pek Sing Choy Lay Fut

- **Lai Hung** — Northern Shaolin, Choy Lay Fut

Glossary

Ch'an	禪	a branch of Buddhism that emphasizes enlightenment through meditation
Ch'en Nien-po	陳年柏	one of the Ten Tigers of Kwangtung
Ch'i	氣	energy that shapes and maintains living organisms
Ch'i kung	氣功	the practice of cultivating and regulating one's ch'i through breathing, motion, and meditation exercises
Ch'ien kung hou chien	前弓後箭	bow stance
Ch'uan	拳	fist
Ch'uan Hsin	穿心	form number four of the ten Pek Sil Lum forms
Cha t'ui	扎腿	rooted stance
Chang	掌	palm
Chiang An	江安	one of Ten Tigers of Kwangtung
Chin chi tu li	金雞獨立	golden chicken stance
Ching Wu	精武	a martial arts association founded by Hu Yuan-chi
Chou Shen-chih	周慎之	one of the Ten Tigers of Kwangtung
Choy Lay Fut	蔡李佛	a southern Chinese martial art
Fan Chung-hsui	樊鐘秀	a Chinese warlord
Feng Yu-hsiang	馮玉祥	a Nationalist general
Fu Chen-sung	傅振嵩	one of the Five Tigers of Northern China
Golden Bell Cover	金鐘罩	a from of ch'i kung designed to enable one's body to withstand strikes and blows
Ho tsui	鶴嘴	crane break
Hsing Yi	形意	a Chinese internal martial art
Hsung feng t'ui	旋風腿	tornado kick
Hu chao	虎爪	tiger claw
Hung T'ou Fo Wei	鴻頭佛尾	a southern Chinese martial art
Hung Gar	洪家	a southern Chinese martial art
Huo Yuan-chia	霍元甲	a famous Chinese martial artist; founder of the Ching Wu

I-Chin Ching	易筋經		Muscle Rehabilitation Classic, a treatise attributed to Bodhidharma
Iron palm	鐵掌		a discipline designed to enable the practitioner to break or penetrate hard objects with his hands
Jih ch'uan	日拳		vertical punch
K'ai men	開門		form number one of the ten Pek Sil Lum forms
Ku Ju-chang	顧汝章		one of the Five Tigers of Northern China; famous Pek Sil Lum, iron palm, and ch'i kung practitioner
Kua shou ch'ui	掛手錘		backfist/roundhouse strike
Kung Fu	功夫		perfection achieved through exertion; informal term to denote a Chinese martial art
Kuo shu	國術		literally, "national art"; a synonym for wu shu
Lai Hung	黎雄		practitioner of Pek Sil Lum and Choy Lay Fut
Lai Kan-ch'ing	賴乾清		one of the Ten Tigers of Kwangtung
Li Ch'ou	李秋		one of the Ten Tigers of Kwangtung; practitioner of Choy Lay Fut
Li Hsien-wu	李先五		one of the Five Tigers of Northern China
Lian Huan	連環		form number nine of the ten Pek Sil Lum forms
Ling Lu	領路		form number two of the Pek Sil Lum forms
Liu Chin-tung	劉錦東		one of the Ten Tigers of Kwangtung
Lun Chih	倫枝		one of the Ten Tigers of Kwangtung
Lung Tze-hsiang	龍子祥		one of the Ten Tigers of Kwangtung; a disciple of Ku Ju-chang
Ma En	馬恩		one of the Ten Tigers of Kwangtung
Mei Hua	梅花		form number seven of the ten Pek Sil Lum forms
Miao Hsing	妙興		an abbot of the Honan Shaolin temple
Nei pai lien t'ui	內擺連腿		inside crescent kick
Niu ma	扭馬		twisting horse stance
Northern Shaolin	北少林		a northern Chinese martial art; also known as Pek Sil Lum
P'an Chu	潘珠		one of the Ten Tigers of Kwangtung
P'i ch'uan	劈拳		cleaving block/strike
P'ing ch'uan	平拳		horizontal strike
Pa Kua	八卦		a Chinese internal martial art

Pa Pu	拔步	form number eight of the ten Pek Sil Lum forms
Pao ch'uan	抱拳	fists held at the ready position
Praying mantis	螳螂	a Chinese martial art
Shih Fa	式法	form number ten of the ten Pek Sil Lum forms
Shuang fei t'ui	雙飛腿	double jumping kick
Ssu p'ing ma	四平馬	a square horse stance
T'ai Ch'i Chiuan	太極拳	a Chinese internal martial art
Tan San	譚三	one of the Five Tigers of Southern China; a practitioner of Choy Lay Fut
T'an T'ui	彈腿	a style of martial art that originated with the Muslim community in China
T'i t'ui	踢腿	toe kick
Teng t'ui	蹬腿	heel kick
Tiao t'i ma	吊蹄馬	rearing horse stance
Tien Hsueh	點穴	the art of attacking pressure and nerve points
Tuan Ta	短打	"short distance fighting"; form number six of the ten Pek Sil Lum forms
Wai pai lien t'ui	外擺連腿	outside crescent kick
Wan Lai-sheng	萬籟聲	one of the five Tigers of Nothern China
Wang Shao-chou	王少周	one of the Ten Tigers of Kwangtung
White Crane	白鶴拳	a Chinese martial art
Wing Ch'un	詠春	a Chinese martial art
Wu kung	武功	a synonym for wu shu
Wu shu	武術	literally, "martial art"
Wu Yi	武藝	form number five of the ten Pek Sil Lum forms
Yeh Yu-t'ing	葉雨亭	a disciple of Huo Yuan-chia
Yen Shang-wu	嚴尚武	a disciple of Ku Ju-chang; practitioner of Pek Sil Lum
Zuo Ma	坐馬	form number three of the ten Pek Sil Lum forms

Endnotes

[1] In Cantonese, Bak or Pek Sil Lum, and in Mandarin, Bei Shaolin.

[2] In Mandarin: K'ai Men, Ling Lu, Zuo Ma, Ch'uan Hsin, Tuan Ta, Wu Yi Pa Pu, Mei Hua, Lian Huan, Shih Fa.

[3] R.L. Rielly, *The History of American Karate* (Little Ferry: Semper Fi Company, Inc., 1973), 3.

[4] Ibid, 4.

[5] Yang Jwing-Ming and Jeffery A. Bolt, *Shaolin Long Fist Kung Fu* (Burbank: Unique Publications, 1982), 7-8.

[6] The Ten Tigers of Kwangtung included Lung Tze-hsiang, Li Ch'ou, Ch'en Nien-po, Liu Chin-tung, Chiang An, Lun Chih, P'an Chu, Ma En, Lai Kan-ch'ing, and Chou Shen-chih.

[7] Harriet Beinfield and Efrem Korngold, *Between Heaven and Earth, A Guide to Chinese Medicine* (New York: Ballantine Books, 1991), 240.

[8] Ibid, 266.

[9] Burton Watson, *Chuang Tze, Basic Writings* (New York: Columbia University Press, 1964), 46-47.